Learning Android App Testing

C000137444

Improve your Android applications through intensive testing and debugging

Paul Blundell

Diego Torres Milano

BIRMINGHAM - MUMBAI

Learning Android Application Testing

Copyright © 2015 Packt Publishing

All rights reserved. No part of this book may be reproduced, stored in a retrieval system, or transmitted in any form or by any means, without the prior written permission of the publisher, except in the case of brief quotations embedded in critical articles or reviews.

Every effort has been made in the preparation of this book to ensure the accuracy of the information presented. However, the information contained in this book is sold without warranty, either express or implied. Neither the authors, nor Packt Publishing, and its dealers and distributors will be held liable for any damages caused or alleged to be caused directly or indirectly by this book.

Packt Publishing has endeavored to provide trademark information about all of the companies and products mentioned in this book by the appropriate use of capitals. However, Packt Publishing cannot guarantee the accuracy of this information.

First published: June 2011

Second edition: March 2015

Production reference: 1240315

Published by Packt Publishing Ltd.
Livery Place
35 Livery Street
Birmingham B3 2PB, UK.

ISBN 978-1-78439-533-9

www.packtpub.com

Credits

Authors
Paul Blundell
Diego Torres Milano

Reviewers
BJ Peter DeLaCruz
Noureddine Dimachk
Miguel L Gonzalez
Henrik Kirk
Sérgio Lima
João Trindade

Commissioning Editor
Taron Pereira

Acquisition Editor
Rebecca Youé

Content Development Editor
Manasi Pandire

Technical Editor
Indrajit A. Das

Copy Editors
Khushnum Mistry
Alfida Paiva
Vikrant Phadke
Adithi Shetty

Project Coordinator
Suzanne Coutinho

Proofreaders
Simran Bhogal
Joanna McMahon

Indexer
Hemangini Bari

Graphics
Valentina D'silva

Production Coordinator
Alwin Roy

Cover Work
Alwin Roy

About the Authors

Paul Blundell is an aspiring software craftsman and senior Android developer at Novoda. Before Novoda, he worked at AutoTrader and Thales, with apps that he released racking up over one million downloads. A strong believer in software craftsmanship, SOLID architecture, clean code, and testing, Paul has used this methodology to successfully nurture and create many Android applications. These include the Tesco launcher app, which was preinstalled for the recently released Hudl2 tablet; MUBI, a unique film streaming service; and the AutoTrader UK car search app.

If anyone wants to provide feedback, you can always tweet to him `@blundell_apps`. He also likes to write, so you can find more material at `http://blog.blundellapps.com/`.

I'd like to thank everyone at Novoda for being great guys/gals and helping each other all the time to learn and develop. Without the atmosphere of craftsmanship and constant learning, my skills and this book would not have been possible. Also, I'd like to thank my girlfriend for her endless patience. Every time she asked me to help her out, I'd give her the excuse of writing my book. Well, no more excuses because it is finished!

I'd like to acknowledge the legacy author of this book Diego Torres Milano for doing a great job. The chapters outlined are down to your insight into the world of testing on Android, and I hope my rewrite lives up to your ideals.

Finally, I'd like to thank all the people who don't know me but from whom I've learnt a lot. If you, as the reader, want a list of other authors for further research, this is it: Kent Beck, Martin Fowler, Robert C Martin, Romain Guy, Reto Meier, Mark Murphy, Eric Evans, Joshua Block, Ward Cunningham, Kevin Rutherford, JB Rainsberger, and Sandro Mancuso.

Diego Torres Milano has been involved with the Android platform since its inception, by the end of 2007, when he started exploring and researching the platform's possibilities, mainly in the areas of user interfaces, unit and acceptance tests, and Test-driven Development.

This is reflected by a number of articles mainly published on his personal blog (http://dtmilano.blogspot.com), and his participation as a lecturer in some conferences and courses, such as Mobile Dev Camp 2008 in Amsterdam (Netherlands) and Japan Linux Symposium 2009 (Tokyo), Droidcon London 2009, and Skillsmatter 2009 (London, UK). He has also authored Android training courses delivered to various companies in Europe.

Previously, he was the founder and developer of several open source projects, mainly CULT Universal Linux Thin Project (http://cult-thinclient.sf.net) and the very successful PXES Universal Linux Thin Client project (that was later acquired by 2X Software, http://www.2x.com). PXES is a Linux-based operating system specialized for thin clients, used by hundreds of thousands of thin clients all over the world. This project has a popularity peak of 35 million hits and 400K downloads from SourceForge in 2005. This project had a dual impact. Big companies in Europe decided to use it because of improved security and efficiency; and organizations, institutions, and schools in some development countries in South America, Africa, and Asia decided to use it because of the minimal hardware requirements, having a huge social impact of providing computers, sometimes recycled ones, to everyone.

Among the other open source projects that he founded are Autoglade, Gnome-tla, and JGlade, and he has contributed to various Linux distributions, such as RedHat, Fedora, and Ubuntu.

He has also given presentations at the LinuxWorld, LinuxTag, GUADEC ES, University of Buenos Aires, and so on.

Diego has also developed software, participated in open source projects, and advised companies worldwide for more than 15 years.

He can be contacted at dtmilano@gmail.com.

About the Reviewers

BJ Peter DeLaCruz graduated with a master's degree in computer science from the University of Hawaii at Manoa. In 2011, he began his career as a software developer at Referentia Systems Inc. in Honolulu, Hawaii. At Referentia, he assisted in the development of the LiveAction product. After working at Referentia for 2.5 years, he was hired as a Java web developer by the University of Hawaii. Between fall 2014 and spring 2015 semesters, he upgraded Laulima (`http://laulima.hawaii.edu`), the learning management system that the university uses for traditional face-to-face, online, and hybrid classes.

BJ holds three Java certifications, including the Oracle Certified Master, Java SE 6 Developer certification.

He is a successful Android developer. As of January 2015, he has published seven Android apps on Google Play. His latest app, Chamorro Dictionary, is an excellent learning tool for the Chamorro language. You can check out his apps at `http://tinyurl.com/google-play-bpd`.

BJ really likes Gradle because it makes building applications very easy. He was a reviewer for *Gradle in Action*.

His hobbies include learning the Japanese language, reading books about Japanese culture, and making YouTube videos. You can contact him at `bj.peter.delacruz@gmail.com`. You can also visit his website at `http://www.bjpeter.com`.

> I want to thank God for giving me the opportunity to review this book. I also want to thank Nikita Michael for inviting me to become a reviewer and Suzanne Coutinho for sending all the chapters to review. Arigatou gozaimasu!

Noureddine Dimachk is a passionate video gamer since birth. Noureddine started building games using The Games Factory when he was just 10 years old.

Today, he leads a multinational team of 17 enthusiastic developers spread across Lebanon, Argentina, and India to build cutting-edge applications that serve millions of concurrent GSM subscribers, in addition to mobile applications.

A geek by nature, Noureddine likes to experiment with new technologies in his spare time, and he's a passionate *Dota 2* player.

> I would like to thank my amazing wife for standing by me and supporting me in my technical ventures.

Miguel L Gonzalez is a Spanish software engineer working in the United Kingdom since 2010. He took his first programming course at the early age of eight, and it has been his main passion and hobby since then. He soon became attracted to the Web and Internet, which lead him to study telecommunications engineering.

He has worked as a researcher in the university, designing accessible hardware and wireless sensor networks, teaching web development, developing a mixture of Java hardware, desktops, and web apps, and is the head of development in an agency. Since the time he arrived in the UK, he has mainly focused on web and native development for mobiles, and he developed a few Android and iOS apps in coANDcoUK. In 2013, he joined BBC to work on iPlayer, BBC's catch-up service. It was here that he became more serious about unit testing, behavioral testing, and how to drive success via continuous integration.

He tries to keep improving his projects, which can be found at `http://github.com/ktzar` and maintain his personal website, `http://mentadreams.com`. Since his son Alex was born, the spare time for side projects has been reduced, but his wife, Dalia, helps him to find time for them. Nevertheless, he's looking forward to playing *Monkey Island*, designing games, playing the guitar, and traveling the world with his offspring in a few years time.

Henrik Kirk holds a master's degree in computer science from Aarhus University and has over 5 years of experience in Android application development. He is curious about new technologies and has been using Scala as well as Java for Android development. He also enjoys optimizing the user experience through speed and responsive design. He is currently employed as the lead developer at Lapio, creating an awesome timing and race experience for athletes in the US and Europe. In his spare time, he races his mountain bike.

Sérgio Lima is a software engineer and an airplane pilot. It's easy to see that he's a very ambitious person with broad and, at the same time, specific interests. He currently works at a Portuguese company that aims to revolutionize the world with telecom and mobile applications. His curriculum started with a master's degree in electronics and telecommunications and he specialized in computer programming and computer vision. After working at some institutions in Portugal, he worked at CERN in Switzerland, before returning to his home country.

He also loves to fly small planes, such as the Piper "Cherokee" and "Tomahawk", from the nearby aerodrome, to see Portugal from above, admire the radiant sceneries of the country, and experience the freedom of flying.

I would like to thank my family and specially my wonderful princess, "Kika", for her patience, support, and love during the process of reviewing this book.

João Trindade is a software developer who specializes in developing Android apps.

Currently, he is part of a startup in Milan that tracks your mobile phone usage and suggests the best tariff plan for your needs.

He completed his PhD in computer engineering at Lisbon Tech and is interested in everything related to mobile development, software testing, docker containers, or cloud computing.

For 6 years he was a researcher involved in multiple international research projects and has published 18 peer reviewed articles.

His twitter handler is @joaotrindade and his personal web page is `http://joaoptrindade.com`.

He contributes to various open source products on GitHub. You can see his profile at `http://github.com/joninvski`.

www.PacktPub.com

Support files, eBooks, discount offers, and more

For support files and downloads related to your book, please visit www.PacktPub.com.

Did you know that Packt offers eBook versions of every book published, with PDF and ePub files available? You can upgrade to the eBook version at www.PacktPub. com and as a print book customer, you are entitled to a discount on the eBook copy. Get in touch with us at service@packtpub.com for more details.

At www.PacktPub.com, you can also read a collection of free technical articles, sign up for a range of free newsletters and receive exclusive discounts and offers on Packt books and eBooks.

http://PacktLib.PacktPub.com

Do you need instant solutions to your IT questions? PacktLib is Packt's online digital book library. Here, you can search, access, and read Packt's entire library of books.

Why subscribe?

- Fully searchable across every book published by Packt
- Copy and paste, print, and bookmark content
- On demand and accessible via a web browser

Free access for Packt account holders

If you have an account with Packt at www.PacktPub.com, you can use this to access PacktLib today and view 9 entirely free books. Simply use your login credentials for immediate access.

Table of Contents

Preface

It doesn't matter how much time you invest in Android design, or even how careful you are when programming, mistakes are inevitable and bugs will appear. This book will help you minimize the impact of these errors in your Android project and increase your development productivity. It will show you the problems that are easily avoided, to help get you quickly to the testing stage.

Android Application Testing Guide is the first and only book providing a practical introduction to the most commonly available techniques, frameworks, and tools to improve the development of your Android applications. Clear, step-by-step instructions show how to write tests for your applications and assure quality control using various methodologies.

The author's experience in applying application testing techniques to real-world projects enables him to share insights on creating professional Android applications.

The book covers the basics of framework support for tests to architectures and techniques such as Test-driven Development, which is an agile component of the software development process and a technique where you will tackle bugs early on. From the most basic unit tests applied to a sample project to more sophisticated performance tests, this book provides a detailed description of the most widely used techniques in the Android testing world in a recipe-based approach.

The author has extensive experience of working on various development projects throughout his professional career. All this research and knowledge has helped create a book that will serve as a useful resource to any developer navigating the world of Android testing.

What this book covers

Chapter 1, Getting Started with Testing, introduces the different types of testing and their applicability to software development projects in general and to Android in particular. It then goes on to cover testing on the Android platform, unit testing and JUnit, creating an Android test project and running tests.

Chapter 2, Understanding Testing with the Android SDK, starts digging a bit deeper to recognize the building blocks available to create the tests. It covers Assertions, TouchUtils, which are intended to test user interfaces, mock objects, instrumentation, and TestCase class hierarchies.

Chapter 3, Baking with Testing Recipes, provides practical examples of different situations you will commonly encounter while applying the disciplines and techniques described before. The examples are presented in a cookbook style so you can adapt and use them for your projects. The recipes cover Android unit tests, activities, applications, databases and ContentProviders, services, UIs, exceptions, parsers, memory leaks, and a look at testing with Espresso.

Chapter 4, Managing Your Android Testing Environment, provides different conditions to run the tests. It starts with the creation of the Android Virtual Devices (AVD) to provide different conditions and configurations for the application under test and runs the tests using the available options. Finally, it introduces monkey as a way to generate simulated events used for testing.

Chapter 5, Discovering Continuous Integration, introduces this agile technique for software engineering and automation that aims to improve the software quality and reduce the time taken to integrate changes by continuously applying integration and testing frequently.

Chapter 6, Practicing Test-driven Development, introduces the Test-driven Development discipline. It starts with a general revision and later on moves to the concepts and techniques closely related to the Android platform. This is a code-intensive chapter.

Chapter 7, Behavior-driven Development, introduces Behavior-driven Development and some concepts, such as the use of a common vocabulary to express the tests and the inclusion of business participants in the software development project.

Chapter 8, Testing and Profiling Performance, introduces a series of concepts related to benchmarking and profiles from traditional logging statement methods to creating Android performance tests and using profiling tools.

Chapter 9, Alternative Testing Tactics, covers adding code coverage to ensure you know what is tested and what isn't, as well as testing on the host's Java Virtual Machine, investigating Fest, Spoon, and the future of Android testing to build upon and expand your Android testing range.

What you need for this book

To be able to follow the examples in the different chapters, you need a common set of software and tools installed and several other components that are described in every chapter in particular, including their respective download locations.

All the examples are based on the following:

- Mac OSX 10.9.4, fully updated
- Java SE version 1.6.0_24 (build 1.6.0_24-b07)
- Android SDK tools, revision 24
- Android SDK platform-tools, revision 21
- SDK platform Android 4.4, API 20
- Android support library, revision 21
- Android Studio IDE, Version: 1.1.0
- Gradle version 2.2.1
- Git version 1.8.5.2

Who this book is for

If you are an Android developer looking to test your applications or optimize your application development process, then this book is for you. No previous experience in application testing is required.

Conventions

In this book, you will find a number of styles of text that distinguish between different kinds of information. Here are some examples of these styles, and an explanation of their meaning.

Code words in text are shown as follows: "To invoke the `am` command we will be using the `adb shell` command".

A block of code is set as follows:

```
dependencies {
    compile project(':dummylibrary')
}
```

When we wish to draw your attention to a particular part of a code block, the relevant lines or items are set in bold:

```
fahrenheitEditNumber
.addTextChangedListener(
newFehrenheitToCelciusWatcher(fahrenheitEditNumber,
  celsiusEditNumber));
}
```

Any command-line input or output is written as follows:

```
junit.framework.ComparisonFailure: expected:<[]> but was:<[123.45]>
at com.blundell.tut.EditNumberTests.testClear(EditNumberTests.java:31)
at java.lang.reflect.Method.invokeNative(Native Method)
at android.test.AndroidTestRunner.runTest(AndroidTestRunner.java:191)
```

New terms and **important words** are shown in bold. Words that you see on the screen, in menus or dialog boxes for example, appear in the text like this: "The first test performs a click on the **Go** button of the Forwarding Activity."

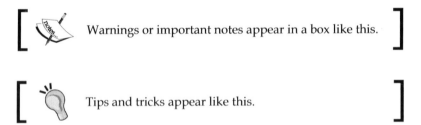

Warnings or important notes appear in a box like this.

Tips and tricks appear like this.

Reader feedback

Feedback from our readers is always welcome. Let us know what you think about this book—what you liked or disliked. Reader feedback is important for us as it helps us develop titles that you will really get the most out of.

To send us general feedback, simply e-mail feedback@packtpub.com, and mention the book's title in the subject of your message.

If there is a topic that you have expertise in and you are interested in either writing or contributing to a book, see our author guide at www.packtpub.com/authors.

Customer support

Now that you are the proud owner of a Packt book, we have a number of things to help you to get the most from your purchase.

Downloading the example code

You can download the example code files from your account at http://www.packtpub.com for all the Packt Publishing books you have purchased. If you purchased this book elsewhere, you can visit http://www.packtpub.com/support and register to have the files e-mailed directly to you.

Errata

Although we have taken every care to ensure the accuracy of our content, mistakes do happen. If you find a mistake in one of our books — maybe a mistake in the text or the code — we would be grateful if you could report this to us. By doing so, you can save other readers from frustration and help us improve subsequent versions of this book. If you find any errata, please report them by visiting http://www.packtpub.com/submit-errata, selecting your book, clicking on the **Errata Submission Form** link, and entering the details of your errata. Once your errata are verified, your submission will be accepted and the errata will be uploaded to our website or added to any list of existing errata under the Errata section of that title.

To view the previously submitted errata, go to https://www.packtpub.com/books/content/support and enter the name of the book in the search field. The required information will appear under the **Errata** section.

Piracy

Piracy of copyrighted material on the Internet is an ongoing problem across all media. At Packt, we take the protection of our copyright and licenses very seriously. If you come across any illegal copies of our works in any form on the Internet, please provide us with the location address or website name immediately so that we can pursue a remedy.

Please contact us at copyright@packtpub.com with a link to the suspected pirated material.

We appreciate your help in protecting our authors and our ability to bring you valuable content.

Questions

If you have a problem with any aspect of this book, you can contact us at questions@packtpub.com, and we will do our best to address the problem.

Questions

You can contact us at questions@packtpub.com if you are having a problem with any aspect of the book, and we will do our best to address it.

1
Getting Started with Testing

Firstly, I will avoid introductions to Android since it is covered in many books already, and I am inclined to believe that if you are reading a book that covers this more advanced topic, you will have already started with Android development.

I will be reviewing the main concepts behind testing, and the techniques, frameworks, and tools available to deploy your testing strategy on Android.

After this overview, we can put the concepts learned into practice. In this chapter we will cover:

- Setting up the infrastructure to test on Android
- Running unit tests using JUnit
- Creating an Android instrumentation test project
- Running multiple tests

We will be creating a simple Android project and its companion tests. The main project will be bare bones so that you can concentrate on the testing components.

I would suggest that new developers with no Android testing experience read this book. If you have more experience with Android projects and have been using testing techniques for them, you might read this chapter as a revision or reaffirmation of the concepts.

Why, what, how, and when to test?

You should understand that early bug detection saves a huge amount of project resources and reduces software maintenance costs. This is the best known reason to write tests for your software development project. Increased productivity will soon be evident.

Additionally, writing tests will give you a deeper understanding of the requirements and the problem to be solved. You will not be able to write tests for a piece of software you don't understand.

This is also the reason behind the approach of writing tests to clearly understand legacy or third-party code and having the testing infrastructure to confidently change or update the codebase.

The more the code is covered by your tests, the higher the likelihood of discovering hidden bugs.

If, during this coverage analysis, you find that some areas of your code are not exercised, additional tests should be added to cover this code as well.

To help in this request, enter Jacoco (`http://www.eclemma.org/jacoco/`), an open source toolkit that measures and reports Java code coverage. It supports various coverage types, as follows:

- Class
- Method
- Block
- Line

Coverage reports can also be obtained in different output formats. Jacoco is supported to some degree by the Android framework, and it is possible to build a Jacoco instrumented version of an Android app.

We will be analyzing the use of Jacoco on Android to guide us to full test coverage of our code in *Chapter 9, Alternative Testing Tactics*.

This screenshot shows how a Jacoco code coverage report is displayed as an HTML file that shows green lines when the code has been tested:

core > com.blundell.tut > TemperatureConverter.java

TemperatureConverter.java

```
1.   package com.blundell.tut;
2.
3.   public final class TemperatureConverter {
4.
5.       static final double ABSOLUTE_ZERO_C = -273.15d;
6.       static final double ABSOLUTE_ZERO_F = -459.67d;
7.
8.       private static final String ERROR_MESSAGE_BELOW_ZERO_FMT = "Invalid temperature: %.2f%c below absolute zero";
9.
10.      private TemperatureConverter() {
11.          // non-instantiable helper class
12.      }
13.
14.      public static double fahrenheitToCelsius(double fahrenheit) {
15.          if (fahrenheit < ABSOLUTE_ZERO_F) {
16.              String msg = String.format(ERROR_MESSAGE_BELOW_ZERO_FMT, fahrenheit, 'F');
17.              throw new InvalidTemperatureException(msg);
18.          }
19.          return ((fahrenheit - 32) / 1.8d);
20.      }
21.
22.      public static double celsiusToFahrenheit(double celsius) {
23.          if (celsius < ABSOLUTE_ZERO_C) {
24.              String msg = String.format(ERROR_MESSAGE_BELOW_ZERO_FMT, celsius, 'C');
25.              throw new InvalidTemperatureException(msg);
26.          }
27.          return (celsius * 1.8d + 32);
28.      }
29.
30.  }
```

By default, the Jacoco gradle plugin isn't supported in Android Studio; therefore, you cannot see code coverage in your IDE, and so code coverage has to be viewed as separate HTML reports. There are other options available with other plugins such as Atlassian's Clover or Eclipse with EclEmma.

Tests should be automated, and you should run some or all tests every time you introduce a change or addition to your code in order to ensure that all the conditions that were met before are still met, and that the new code satisfies the tests as expected.

This leads us to the introduction of **Continuous Integration**, which will be discussed in detail in *Chapter 5, Discovering Continuous Integration*, enabling the automation of tests and the building process.

If you don't use automated testing, it is practically impossible to adopt Continuous Integration as part of the development process, and it is very difficult to ensure that changes would not break existing code.

Having tests stops you from introducing new bugs into already completed features when you touch the code base. These regressions are easily done, and tests are a barrier to this happening. Further, you can now catch and find problems at compile time, that is, when you are developing, rather than receiving them as feedback when your users start complaining.

What to test

Strictly speaking, you should test every statement in your code, but this also depends on different criteria and can be reduced to testing the main path of execution or just some key methods. Usually, there's no need to test something that can't be broken; for example, it usually makes no sense to test getters and setters as you probably won't be testing the Java compiler on your own code, and the compiler would have already performed its tests.

In addition to your domain-specific functional areas that you should test, there are some other areas of an Android application that you should consider. We will be looking at these in the following sections.

Activity lifecycle events

You should test whether your activities handle lifecycle events correctly.

If your activity should save its state during the `onPause()` or `onDestroy()` events and later be able to restore it in `onCreate(Bundle savedInstanceState)`, then you should be able to reproduce and test all these conditions and verify that the state was correctly saved and restored.

Configuration change events should also be tested as some of these events cause the current Activity to be recreated. You should test whether the handling of the event is correct and that the newly created Activity preserves the previous state. Configuration changes are triggered even by a device rotation, so you should test your application's ability to handle these situations.

Database and filesystem operations

Database and filesystem operations should be tested to ensure that the operations and any errors are handled correctly. These operations should be tested in isolation at the lower system level, at a higher level through `ContentProviders`, or from the application itself.

To test these components in isolation, Android provides some mock objects in the `android.test.mock` package. A simple way to think of a mock is as a drop-in replacement for the real object, where you have more control of the object's behavior.

Physical characteristics of the device

Before shipping your application, you should be sure that all of the different devices it can be run on are supported, or at least you should detect the unsupported situation and take pertinent measures.

The characteristics of the devices that you should test are:

- Network capabilities
- Screen densities
- Screen resolutions
- Screen sizes
- Availability of sensors
- Keyboard and other input devices
- GPS
- External storage

In this respect, an Android emulator can play an important role because it is practically impossible to have access to all of the devices with all of the possible combinations of features, but you can configure emulators for almost every situation. However, as mentioned before, leave your final tests for actual devices where the real users will run the application so you get feedback from a real environment.

Types of tests

Testing comes in a variety of frameworks with differing levels of support from the Android SDK and your IDE of choice. For now, we are going to concentrate on how to test Android apps using the instrumented Android testing framework, which has full SDK and ASide support, and later on, we will discuss the alternatives.

Testing can be implemented at any time in the development process, depending on the test method employed. However, we will be promoting testing at an early stage of the development cycle, even before the full set of requirements has been defined and the coding process has been started.

There are several types of tests depending on the code being tested. Regardless of its type, a test should verify a condition and return the result of this evaluation as a single Boolean value that indicates its success or failure.

Unit tests

Unit tests are tests written by programmers for other programmers, and they should isolate the component under tests and be able to test it in a repeatable way. That's why unit tests and mock objects are usually placed together. You use mock objects to isolate the unit from its dependencies, to monitor interactions, and also to be able to repeat the test any number of times. For example, if your test deletes some data from a database, you probably don't want the data to be actually deleted and, therefore, not found the next time the test is ran.

JUnit is the de facto standard for unit tests on Android. It's a simple open source framework for automating unit testing, originally written by Erich Gamma and Kent Beck.

Android test cases use JUnit 3 (this is about to change to JUnit 4 in an impending Google release, but as of the time of this writing, we are showing examples with JUnit 3). This version doesn't have annotations, and uses introspection to detect the tests.

A typical Android-instrumented JUnit test would be something like this:

```java
public class MyUnitTestCase extends TestCase {

    public MyUnitTestCase() {
        super("testSomething");
    }

    public void testSomething() {
        fail("Test not implemented yet");
    }
}
```

> You can download the example code files for all Packt books you have purchased from your account at http://www.packtpub.com. If you purchased this book elsewhere, you can visit http://www.packtpub.com/support and register to have the files e-mailed directly to you.

The following sections explain the components that can be used to build up a test case. Note that these components and the pattern of working with a test case are not unique to unit tests, and they can be deployed for the other test types that we will discuss in the following sections.

The setUp() method

This method is called to initialize the fixture (fixture being the test and its surrounding code state).

Overriding it, you have the opportunity to create objects and initialize fields that will be used by tests. It's worth noting that this setup occurs *before* every test.

The tearDown() method

This method is called to finalize the fixture.

Overriding it, you can release resources used by the initialization or tests. Again, this method is invoked *after* every test.

For example, you can release a database or close a network connection here.

There are more methods you can hook into before and after your test methods, but these are used rarely, and will be explained as we bump into them.

Outside the test method

JUnit is designed in a way that the entire tree of test instances is built in one pass, and then the tests are executed in a second pass. Therefore, the test runner holds strong references to all test instances for the duration of the test execution. This means that for very large and very long test runs with many Test instances, none of the tests may be garbage collected until the entire test is run. This is particularly important in Android and while testing on limited devices as some tests may fail not because of an intrinsic failure but because of the amount of memory needed to run the application, in addition to its tests exceeding the device limits.

Therefore, if you allocate external or limited resources in a test, such as `Services` or `ContentProviders`, you are responsible for freeing those resources. Explicitly setting an object to null in the `tearDown()` method, for example, allows it to be garbage collected before the end of the entire test run.

Inside the test method

All `public void` methods whose names start with `test` will be considered as a test. As opposed to JUnit 4, JUnit 3 doesn't use annotations to discover the tests; instead, it uses introspection to find their names. There are some annotations available in the Android test framework such as `@SmallTest`, `@MediumTest`, or `@LargeTest`, which don't turn a simple method into a test but organize them in different categories. Ultimately, you will have the ability to run tests for a single category using the test runner.

As a rule of thumb, name your tests in a descriptive way and use nouns and the condition being tested. Also, remember to test for exceptions and wrong values instead of just testing positive cases.

For example, some valid tests and naming could be:

- `testOnCreateValuesAreLoaded()`
- `testGivenIllegalArgumentThenAConversionErrorIsThrown()`
- `testConvertingInputToStringIsValid()`

During the execution of the test, some conditions, side effects, or method returns should be compared against the expectations. To ease these operations, JUnit provides a full set of `assert*` methods to compare the expected results from the test to the actual results after running them, throwing exceptions if the conditions are not met. Then, the test runner handles these exceptions and presents the results.

These methods, which are overloaded to support different arguments, include:

- `assertTrue()`
- `assertFalse()`
- `assertEquals()`
- `assertNull()`
- `assertNotNull()`
- `assertSame()`
- `assertNotSame()`
- `fail()`

In addition to these JUnit assert methods, Android extends Assert in two specialized classes, providing additional tests:

- `MoreAsserts`
- `ViewAsserts`

Mock objects

Mock objects are mimic objects used instead of calling the real domain objects to enable testing units in isolation.

Generally, this is accomplished to verify that the correct methods are called, but they can also be of great help to isolate your tests from the surrounding code and be able to run the tests independently and ensure repeatability.

The Android testing framework supports mock objects that you will find very useful when writing tests. You need to provide some dependencies to be able to compile the tests. There are also external libraries that can be used when mocking.

Several classes are provided by the Android testing framework in the `android.test.mock` package:

- `MockApplication`
- `MockContentProvider`
- `MockContentResolver`
- `MockContext`
- `MockCursor`
- `MockDialogInterface`
- `MockPackageManager`
- `MockResources`

Almost any component of the platform that could interact with your Activity can be created by instantiating one of these classes.

However, they are not real implementations but stubs, the idea being you extend one of these classes to create a real mock object and override the methods you want to implement. Any methods you do not override will throw an `UnsupportedOperationException`.

Integration tests

Integration tests are designed to test the way individual components work together. Modules that have been unit tested independently are now combined together to test the integration.

Usually, Android Activities require some integration with the system infrastructure to be able to run. They need the Activity lifecycle provided by the `ActivityManager`, and access to resources, the filesystem, and databases.

The same criteria apply to other Android components such as `Services` or `ContentProviders` that need to interact with other parts of the system to achieve their duty.

In all these cases, there are specialized test classes provided by the Android testing framework that facilitates the creation of tests for these components.

UI tests

User Interface tests test the visual representation of your application, such as how a dialog looks or what UI changes are made when a dialog is dismissed.

Special considerations should be taken if your tests involve UI components. As you may have already known, only the main thread is allowed to alter the UI in Android. Thus, a special annotation `@UIThreadTest` is used to indicate that a particular test should be run on that thread and it would have the ability to alter the UI. On the other hand, if you only want to run parts of your test on the UI thread, you may use the `Activity.runOnUiThread(Runnable r)` method that provides the corresponding `Runnable`, which contains the testing instructions.

A helper class `TouchUtils` is also provided to aid in the UI test creation, allowing the generation of the following events to send to the Views, such as:

- Click
- Drag
- Long click
- Scroll
- Tap
- Touch

By these means, you can actually remote control your application from the tests. Also, Android has recently introduced Espresso for UI instrumented tests, and we will be covering this in *Chapter 3, Baking with Testing Recipes*.

Functional or acceptance tests

In agile software development, functional or acceptance tests are usually created by business and Quality Assurance (QA) people, and expressed in a business domain language. These are high-level tests to assert the completeness and correctness of a user story or feature. They are created ideally through collaboration between business customers, business analysts, QA, testers, and developers. However, the business customers (product owners) are the primary owners of these tests.

Some frameworks and tools can help in this field, such as Calabash (http://calaba.sh) or most notably FitNesse (http://www.fitnesse.org), which can be easily integrated, up to some point, into the Android development process, and will let you create acceptance tests and check their results as follows:

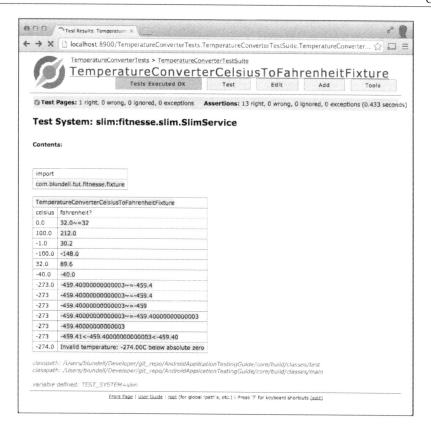

Lately, within acceptance testing, a new trend named **Behavior-driven Development** has gained some popularity, and in a very brief description, it can be understood as a cousin of Test-driven Development. It aims to provide a common vocabulary between business and technology people in order to increase mutual understanding.

Behavior-driven Development can be expressed as a framework of activities based on three principles (more information can be found at http://behaviour-driven.org):

- Business and technology should refer to the same system in the same way
- Any system should have an identified, verifiable value to the business
- Upfront analysis, design, and planning, all have a diminishing return

To apply these principles, business people are usually involved in writing test case scenarios in a high-level language and use a tool such as **jbehave** (http://jbehave.org). In the following example, these scenarios are translated into Java code that expresses the same test scenario.

Test case scenario

As an illustration of this technique, here is an oversimplified example.

The scenario, as written by a product owner, is as follows:

```
Given I'm using the Temperature Converter.
When I enter 100 into Celsius field.
Then I obtain 212 in Fahrenheit field.
```

It would be translated into something similar to:

```
@Given("I am using the Temperature Converter")
public void createTemperatureConverter() {
    // do nothing this is syntactic sugar for readability
}

@When("I enter $celsius into Celsius field")
public void setCelsius(int celsius) {
    this.celsius = celsius;
}

@Then("I obtain $fahrenheit in Fahrenheit field")
public void testCelsiusToFahrenheit(int fahrenheit) {
    assertEquals(fahrenheit,
                TemperatureConverter.celsiusToFahrenheit(celsius));
}
```

This allows both the programmers and the business users to speak the language of the domain (in this case, temperature conversions), and both are able to relate it back to their day-to-day work.

Performance tests

Performance tests measure performance characteristics of the components in a repeatable way. If performance improvements are required by some part of the application, the best approach is to measure performance before and after a change is introduced.

As is widely known, premature optimization does more harm than good, so it is better to clearly understand the impact of your changes on the overall performance.

The introduction of the **Dalvik JIT** compiler in Android 2.2 changed some optimization patterns that were widely used in Android development. Nowadays, every recommendation about performance improvements in the Android developer's site is backed up by performance tests.

System tests

The system is tested as a whole, and the interaction between the components, software, and hardware is exercised. Normally, system tests include additional classes of tests such as:

- GUI tests
- Smoke tests
- Mutation tests
- Performance tests
- Installation tests

Android Studio and other IDE support

JUnit is fully supported by Android Studio, and it lets you create tested Android projects. Furthermore, you can run the tests and analyze the results without leaving the IDE (to some extent).

This also provides a more subtle advantage; being able to run the tests from the IDE allows you to debug the tests that are not behaving correctly.

In the following screenshot, we can see how ASide runs **19 unit tests**, taking 1.043 seconds, with **0 Errors** and **0 Failure**s detected. The name of each test and its duration is also displayed. If there were a failure, the **Failure Trace** would show the related information, as shown in the following screenshot:

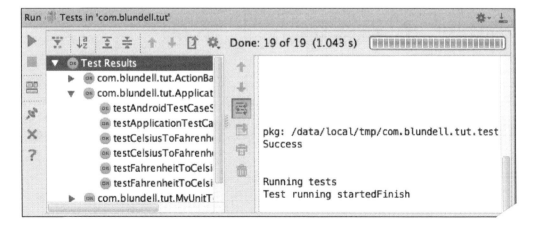

There is also Android support in Eclipse IDE using the Android Development Tools plugin.

Even if you are not developing in an IDE, you can find support to run the tests with gradle (check http://gradle.org if you are not familiar with this tool). The tests are run using the command gradle connectedAndroidTest. This will install and run the tests for the debug build on a connected Android device.

This is actually the same method that Android Studio uses under the hood. ASide will just run the Gradle commands to build the project and run the tests, although with selective compilation.

Java testing framework

The Java testing framework is the backbone of Android testing, and sometimes, you can get away without writing Android-specific code. This can be a good thing, because as we continue on our testing quest, you will notice that we deploy Android framework tests to a device, and this has an impact on the speed of our tests, that is, the speed we get feedback from a pass or a fail.

If you architect your app in a clever way, you can create pure Java classes that can be tested in isolation away from Android. The two main benefits of this are increased speed of feedback from test results, and also, to quickly plug together libraries and code snippets to create powerful test suites, you can use the near ten years of experience of other programmers doing Java testing.

Android testing framework

Android provides a very advanced testing framework that extends the industry standard JUnit library with specific features that are suitable to implement all of the testing strategies and types we mentioned before. In some cases, additional tools are needed, but the integration of these tools is, in most of the cases, simple and straightforward.

Most relevant key features of the Android testing environment include:

- Android extensions to the JUnit framework that provide access to Android system objects

- An instrumentation framework that lets the tests control and examine the application

- Mock versions of commonly used Android system objects
- Tools to run single tests or test suites, with or without instrumentation
- Support to manage tests and test projects in Android Studio and at the command line

Instrumentation

The instrumentation framework is the foundation of the testing framework. Instrumentation controls the application under tests and permits the injection of mock components required by the application to run. For example, you can create mock Contexts before the application starts and let the application use it.

All the interactions of the application with the surrounding environment can be controlled using this approach. You can also isolate your application in a restricted environment to be able to predict the results that force the values returned by some methods, or that mock persistent and unchanged data for the ContentProvider's databases or even the filesystem content.

A standard Android project has its instrumentation tests in a correlated source folder called androidTest. This creates a separate application that runs tests on your application. There is no AndroidManifest here as it is automatically generated. The instrumentation can be customized inside the Android closure of your build. gradle file, and these changes are reflected in the autogenerated AndroidManifest. However, you can still run your tests with the default settings if you choose to change nothing.

Examples of things you can change are the test application package name, your test runner, or how to toggle performance-testing features:

```
testApplicationId "com.blundell.something.non.default"
testInstrumentationRunner  "com.blundell.tut.CustomTestRunner"
testHandleProfiling false
testFunctionalTest true
testCoverageEnabled true
```

Here, the Instrumentation package (testApplicationId) is a different package to the main application. If you don't change this yourself, it will default to your main application package with the .test suffix added.

Then, the Instrumentation test runner is declared, which can be helpful if you create custom annotations to allow special behavior; for example, each test runs twice upon failure. In the case of not declaring a runner, the default custom runner android. test.InstrumentationTestRunner is used.

At the moment, `testHandleProfiling` and `testFunctionalTest` are undocumented and unused, so watch out for when we are told what we can do with these. Setting `testCoverageEnabled` to true will allow you to gather code coverage reports using Jacoco. We will come back to this later.

Also, notice that both the application being tested and the tests themselves are Android applications with their corresponding APKs installed. Internally, they will be sharing the same process and thus have access to the same set of features.

When you run a test application, the **Activity Manager** (`http://developer. android.com/intl/de/reference/android/app/ActivityManager.html`) uses the instrumentation framework to start and control the test runner, which in turn uses instrumentation to shut down any running instances of the main application, starts the test application, and then starts the main application in the same process. This allows various aspects of the test application to work directly with the main application.

Gradle

Gradle is an advanced build toolkit that allows you to manage dependencies and define a custom login to build your project. The Android build system is a plugin on top of Gradle, and this is what gives you the domain-specific language discussed previously such as setting a `testInstrumentationRunner`.

The idea of using Gradle is that it allows you to build your Android apps from the command line for machines without using an IDE such as a continuous integration machine. Also, with first line integration of Gradle into the building of projects in Android Studio, you get the exact same custom build configuration from the IDE or command line.

Other benefits include being able to customize and extend the build process; for example, each time your CI builds your project, you could automatically upload a beta APK to the Google play store. You can create multiple APKs with different features using the same project, for example, one version that targets Google play in an app purchase and another that targets the Amazon app store's coin payments.

Gradle and the Android Gradle plugin make for a powerful combination, and so, we will be using this build framework throughout the rest of the samples in this book.

Test targets

During the evolution of your development project, your tests would be targeted to different devices. From simplicity, flexibility, and speed of testing on an emulator to the unavoidable final testing on the specific device you are intending your application to be run upon, you should be able to run your application on all of them.

There are also some intermediate cases such as running your tests on a local JVM virtual machine, on the development computer, or on a **Dalvik** virtual machine or Activity, depending on the case.

Every case has its pros and cons, but the good news is that you have all of these alternatives available to run your tests.

The emulator is probably the most powerful target as you can modify almost every parameter from its configuration to simulate different conditions for your tests. Ultimately, your application should be able to handle all of these situations, so it's much better to discover the problems upfront than when the application has been delivered.

The real devices are a requirement for performance tests, as it is somewhat difficult to extrapolate performance measurements from a simulated device. You will enjoy the real user experience only when using the real device. Rendering, scrolling, flinging, and other cases should be tested before delivering the application.

Creating the Android project

We will create a new Android project. This is done from the ASide menu by going to **File | New Project**. This then leads us through the wysiwyg guide to create a project.

In this particular case, we are using the following values for the required component names (clicking on the **Next** button in between screens):

- Application name: AndroidApplicationTestingGuide
- Company domain: blundell.com
- Form factor: Phone and Tablet
- Minimum SDK: 17
- Add an Activity: Blank Activity (go with default names)

The following screenshot shows the start of the form editor for reference:

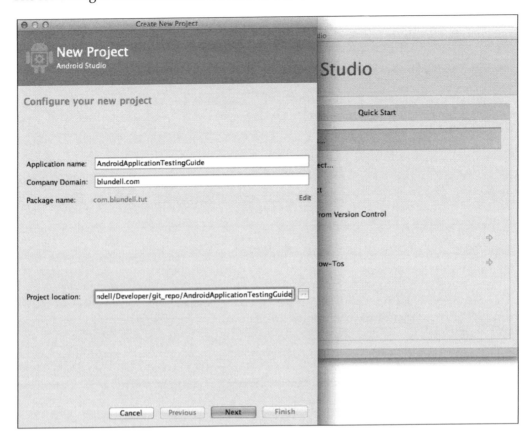

When you click on **Finish** and the application is created, it will automatically generate the androidTest source folder under the app/src directory, and this is where you can add your instrumented test cases.

> Alternatively, to create an androidTest folder for an existing Gradle Android project, you can select the src folder and then go to **File | New | Directory**. Then, write androidTest/java in the dialog prompt. When the project rebuilds, the path will then automatically be added so that you can create tests.

Package explorer

After having created our project, the project view should look like one of the images shown in the following screenshot. This is because ASide has multiple ways to show the project outline. On the left, we can note the existence of the two source directories, one colored green for the test source and the other blue for the project source. On the right, we have the new Android project view that tries to simplify the hierarchy by compressing useless and merging functionally similar folders.

Now that we have the basic infrastructure set up, it's time for us to start adding some tests, as shown in the following screenshot:

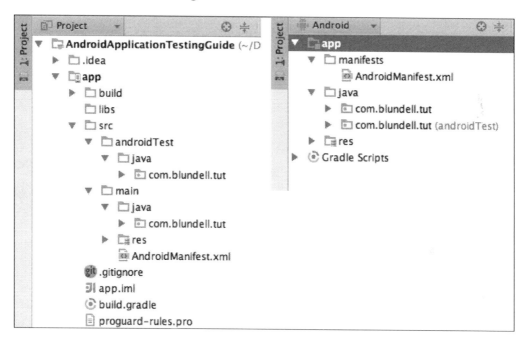

There's nothing to test right now, but as we are setting up the fundamentals of a Test-driven Development discipline, we are adding a dummy test just to get acquainted with the technique.

The `src/androidTest/java` folder in your `AndroidApplicationTestingGuide` project is the perfect place to add the tests. You could declare a different folder if you really wanted to, but we're sticking to defaults. The package should be the same as the corresponding package of the component being tested.

Right now, we are not concentrating on the content of the tests but on the concepts and placement of those tests.

Creating a test case

As described before, we are creating our test cases in the `src/androidTest/java` folder of the project.

You can create the file manually by right-clicking on the package and selecting New... | Java Class. However, in this particular case, we'll take advantage of ASide to create our JUnit TestCase. Open the class under test (in this case, MainActivity) and hover over the class name until you see a lightbulb (or press *Ctrl/Command* + 1). Select **Create Test** from the menu that appears.

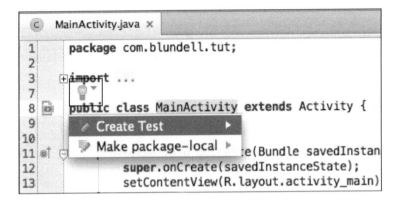

These are the values that we should enter when we create the test case:

- **Testing library**: JUnit 3
- **Class name**: MainActivityTest
- **Superclass**: junit.framework.TestCase
- **Destination package**: com.blundell.tut
- **Superclass**: junit.framework.TestCase
- **Generate**: Select none

After entering all the required values, our JUnit test case creation dialog would look like this.

As you can see, you could also have checked one of the methods of the class to generate an empty test method stub. These stub methods may be useful in some cases, but you have to consider that testing should be a behavior-driven process rather than a method-driven one.

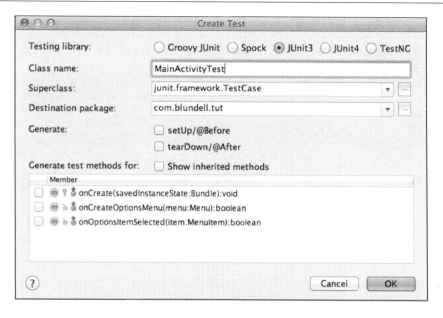

The basic infrastructure for our tests is in place; what is left is to add a dummy test to verify that everything is working as expected. We now have a test case template, so the next step is to start completing it to suit our needs. To do it, open the recently created test class and add the `testSomething()` test.

We should have something like this:

```
package com.blundell.tut;

import android.test.suitebuilder.annotation.SmallTest;

import junit.framework.TestCase;

public class MainActivityTest extends TestCase {

    public MainActivityTest() {
        super("MainActivityTest");
    }

    @SmallTest
    public void testSomething() throws Exception {
        fail("Not implemented yet");
    }
}
```

> The no-argument constructor is needed to run a specific test from the command line, as explained later using am instrumentation.

This test will always fail, presenting the message: **Not implemented yet**. In order to do this, we will use the fail method from the `junit.framework.Assert` class that fails the test with the given message.

Test annotations

Looking carefully at the test definition, you might notice that we decorated the test using the `@SmallTest` annotation, which is a way to organize or categorize our tests and run them separately.

There are other annotations that can be used by the tests, such as:

Annotation	Description
`@SmallTest`	Marks a test that should run as part of the small tests.
`@MediumTest`	Marks a test that should run as part of the medium tests.
`@LargeTest`	Marks a test that should run as part of the large tests.
`@Smoke`	Marks a test that should run as part of the smoke tests. The `android.test.suitebuilder.SmokeTestSuiteBuilder` will run all tests with this annotation.
`@FlakyTest`	Use this annotation on the `InstrumentationTestCase` class' test methods. When this is present, the test method is re-executed if the test fails. The total number of executions is specified by the tolerance, and defaults to 1. This is useful for tests that may fail due to an external condition that could vary with time. For example, to specify a tolerance of 4, you would annotate your test with: `@FlakyTest(tolerance=4)`.

Annotation	Description
@UIThreadTest	Use this annotation on the `InstrumentationTestCase` class' test methods. When this is present, the test method is executed on the application's main thread (or UI thread).
	As instrumentation methods may not be used when this annotation is present, there are other techniques if, for example, you need to modify the UI and get access to the instrumentation within the same test.

	In such cases, you can resort to the `Activity.runOnUIThread()` method that allows you to create any Runnable and run it in the UI thread from within your test:
	 ```mActivity.runOnUIThread(new Runnable() {```
	 ```public void run() {```
	 ```// do somethings```
	 ```}```
	 ```});```

@Suppress	Use this annotation on test classes or test methods that should not be included in a test suite.
	This annotation can be used at the class level, where none of the methods in that class are included in the test suite, or at the method level, to exclude just a single method or a set of methods.

Now that we have the tests in place, it's time to run them, and that's what we are going to do next.

Running the tests

There are several ways of running our tests, and we will analyze them here.

Additionally, as mentioned in the previous section about annotations, tests can be grouped or categorized and run together, depending on the situation.

Running all tests from Android Studio

This is perhaps the simplest method if you have adopted ASide as your development environment. This will run all the tests in the package.

Select the app module in your project and then go to **Run | (android icon) All Tests**.

If a suitable device or emulator is not found, you will be asked to start or connect one.

The tests are then run, and the results are presented inside the Run perspective, as shown in the following screenshot:

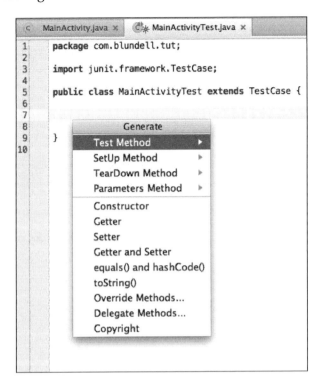

A more detailed view of the results and the messages produced during their execution can also be obtained in the LogCat view within the Android DDMS perspective, as shown in the following screenshot:

Running a single test case from your IDE

There is an option to run a single test case from ASide, should you need to. Open the file where the test resides, right-click on the method name you want to run, and just like you run all the tests, select **Run | (android icon) testMethodName**.

When you run this, as usual, only this test will be executed. In our case, we have only one test, so the result will be similar to the screenshot presented earlier.

> Running a single test like this is a shortcut that actually creates a run configuration for you that is specific to that one method. If you want to look into the details of this, from the menu, select **Run | Edit Configurations**, and under **Android Tests**, you should be able to see a configuration with the name of the test you just executed.

Running from the emulator

The default system image used by the emulator has the Dev Tools application installed, providing several handy tools and settings. Among these tools, we can find a rather long list, as is shown in the following screenshot:

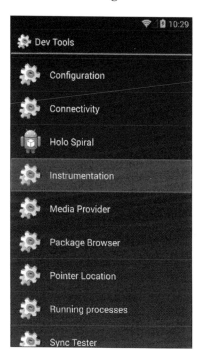

Now, we are interested in **Instrumentation**, which is the way to run our tests. This application lists all of the packages installed that define instrumentation tag tests in their project. We can run the tests by selecting our tests based on the package name, as shown in the following screenshot:

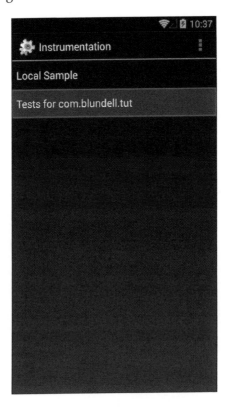

When the tests are run in this way, the results can be seen through DDMS / LogCat, as described in the previous section.

Running tests from the command line

Finally, tests can be run from the command line too. This is useful if you want to automate or script the process.

To run the tests, we use the am instrument command (strictly speaking, the am command and instrument subcommand), which allows us to run instrumentations specifying the package name and some other options.

You might wonder what "am" stands for. It is short for Activity Manager, a main component of the internal Android infrastructure that is started by the System Server at the beginning of the boot process, and it is responsible for managing Activities and their life cycle. Additionally, as we can see here, it is also responsible for Activity instrumentation.

The general usage of the am instrument command is:

```
am instrument [flags] <COMPONENT> -r -e <NAME> <VALUE> -p <FILE>-w
```

This table summarizes the most common options:

Option	Description
`-r`	Prints raw results. This is useful to collect raw performance data.
`-e <NAME> <VALUE>`	Sets arguments by name. We will examine its usage shortly. This is a generic option argument that allows us to set the <name, value> pairs.
`-p <FILE>`	Writes profiling data to an external file.
`-w`	Waits for instrumentation to finish before exiting. This is normally used in commands. Although not mandatory, it's very handy, as otherwise, you will not be able to see the test's results.

To invoke the am command, we will be using the adb shell command or, if you already have a shell running on an emulator or device, you can issue the am command directly in the shell command prompt.

Running all tests

This command line will open the adb shell and then run all tests with the exception of performance tests:

```
$: adb shell
#: am instrument -w com.blundell.tut.test/android.test.
InstrumentationTestRunner

com.blundell.tut.MainActivityTest:
```

Failure in `testSomething`:

```
junit.framework.AssertionFailedError: Not implemented yet


at com.blundell.tut.MainActivityTest.testSomething(MainActivityTest.
java:15)
at java.lang.reflect.Method.invokeNative(Native Method)
at android.test.AndroidTestRunner.runTest(AndroidTestRunner.java:191)
at android.test.AndroidTestRunner.runTest(AndroidTestRunner.java:176)
at android.test.InstrumentationTestRunner.onStart
               (InstrumentationTestRunner.java:554)
at android.app.Instrumentation$InstrumentationThread.run
               (Instrumentation.java:1701)


Test results for InstrumentationTestRunner=.F
Time: 0.002


FAILURES!!!
Tests run: 1,  Failures: 1,  Errors: 0
```

Note that the package you declare with –w is the package of your instrumentation tests, not the package of the application under test.

Running tests from a specific test case

To run all the tests in a specific test case, you can use:

```
$: adb shell
#: am instrument -w -e class com.blundell.tut.MainActivityTest com.
blundell.tut.test/android.test.InstrumentationTestRunner
```

Running a specific test by name

Additionally, we have the alternative of specifying which test we want to run in the command line:

```
$: adb shell
#: am instrument -w -e class com.blundell.tut.
MainActivityTest\#testSomething com.blundell.tut.test/android.test.
InstrumentationTestRunner
```

This test cannot be run in this way unless we have a no-argument constructor in our test case; that is the reason we added it before.

Running specific tests by category

As mentioned before, tests can be grouped into different categories using annotations (Test Annotations), and you can run all tests in this category.

The following options can be added to the command line:

Option	Description
`-e unit true`	This runs all unit tests. These are tests that are not derived from `InstrumentationTestCase` (and are not performance tests).
`-e func true`	This runs all functional tests. These are tests that are derived from `InstrumentationTestCase`.
`-e perf true`	This includes performance tests.
`-e size {small	medium	large}`	This runs small, medium, or large tests depending on the annotations added to the tests.
`-e annotation <annotation-name>`	This runs tests annotated with this annotation. This option is mutually exclusive with the size option.

In our example, we annotated the test method `testSomething()` with `@SmallTest`. So this test is considered to be in that category, and is thus run eventually with other tests that belong to that same category, when we specify the test size as small.

This command line will run all the tests annotated with `@SmallTest`:

```
$: adb shell
#: am instrument -w -e size small com.blundell.tut.test/android.test.
InstrumentationTestRunner
```

Running tests using Gradle

Your gradle build script can also help you run the tests and this will actually do the previous commands under the hood. Gradle can run your tests with this command:

```
gradle connectedAndroidTest
```

Creating a custom annotation

In case you decide to sort the tests by a criterion other than their size, a custom annotation can be created and then specified in the command line.

As an example, let's say we want to arrange our tests according to their importance, so we create an annotation @VeryImportantTest, which we will use in any class where we write tests (MainActivityTest for example):

```
package com.blundell.tut;

/**
 * Marker interface to segregate important tests
 */
@Retention(RetentionPolicy.RUNTIME)
public @interface VeryImportantTest {
}
```

Following this, we can create another test and annotate it with @VeryImportantTest:

```
@VeryImportantTest
public void testOtherStuff() {
fail("Also not implemented yet");
}
```

So, as we mentioned before, we can include this annotation in the am instrument command line to run only the annotated tests:

```
$: adb shell
```

```
#: am instrument -w -e annotation com.blundell.tut.VeryImportantTest com.
blundell.tut.test/android.test. InstrumentationTestRunner
```

Running performance tests

We will be reviewing performance test details in *Chapter 8, Testing and Profiling Performance,* but here, we will introduce the available options to the am instrument command.

To include performance tests on your test run, you should add this command line option:

- -e perf true: This includes performance tests

Dry run

Sometimes, you might only need to know what tests will be run instead of actually running them.

This is the option you need to add to your command line:

- -e log true: This displays the tests to be run instead of running them

This is useful if you are writing scripts around your tests or perhaps building other tools.

Debugging tests

You should assume that your tests might have bugs too. In such a case, usual debugging techniques apply, for example, adding messages through LogCat.

If a more sophisticated debugging technique is needed, you should attach the debugger to the test runner.

In order to do this without giving up on the convenience of the IDE and not having to remember hard-to-memorize command-line options, you can **Debug Run** your run configurations. Thus, you can set a breakpoint in your tests and use it. To toggle a breakpoint, you can select the desired line in the editor and left-click on the margin.

Once it is done, you will be in a standard debugging session, and the debug window should be available to you.

It is also possible to debug your tests from the command line; you can use code instructions to wait for your debugger to attach. We won't be using this command; if you want more details, they can be found at (http://developer.android.com/reference/android/test/InstrumentationTestRunner.html).

Other command-line options

The am instrument command accepts other <name, value> pairs beside the previously mentioned ones:

Name	Value
debug	true. Set break points in your code.
package	This is a fully qualified package name of one or several packages in the test application.
class	A fully qualified test case class to be executed by the test runner. Optionally, this could include the test method name separated from the class name by a hash (#).
coverage	true. Runs the EMMA code coverage and writes the output to a file that can also be specified. We will dig into the details about supporting EMMA code coverage for our tests in *Chapter 9, Alternative Testing Tactics.*

Summary

We have reviewed the main techniques and tools behind testing on Android. Having acquired this knowledge, it will let us begin our journey so that we can start exploiting the benefits of testing in our software development projects.

So far, we have visited the following subjects:

- We briefly analyzed the whys, whats, hows, and whens of testing. Henceforth, we will concentrate more on exploring the hows, now that you're giving testing the importance it deserves.
- We enumerated the different and most common types of tests you would need in your projects, described some of the tools we can count on our testing toolbox, and provided an introductory example of a JUnit unit test to better understand what we are discussing.
- We also created our first Android project with tests, using the Android Studio IDE and Gradle.
- We also created a simple test class to test the Activity in our project. We haven't added any useful test cases yet, but adding those simple ones was intended to validate our infrastructure.
- We also ran this simple test from our IDE and from the command line to understand the alternatives we have. In this process, we mentioned the Activity Manager and its command line incarnation am.
- We created a custom annotation to sort our tests and demonstrate how we can separate or differentiate suites of tests.

In the next chapter, we will start analyzing the mentioned techniques, frameworks, and tools in much greater detail, and provide examples of their usage.

2
Understanding Testing with the Android SDK

We now know how to create tests inside an Android project and how to run these tests. It is now time to start digging a bit deeper to recognize the building blocks available to create more useful tests.

In this second chapter, we will be covering the following topics:

- Common assertions
- View assertions
- Other assertion types
- Helpers to test User Interfaces
- Mock objects
- Instrumentation
- TestCase class hierarchies
- Using external libraries

We will be analyzing these components and showing examples of their use when applicable. The examples in this chapter are intentionally split from the original Android project that contains them. This is done to let you concentrate and focus only on the subject being presented, though the complete examples in a single project can be downloaded as explained later. Right now, we are interested in the trees and not the forest.

Along with the examples presented, we will be identifying reusable common patterns that will help you in the creation of tests for your own projects.

The demonstration application

A very simple application has been created to demonstrate the use of some of the tests in this chapter. The source for the application can be downloaded from XXXXXXXXXXXXXX.

The following screenshot shows this application running:

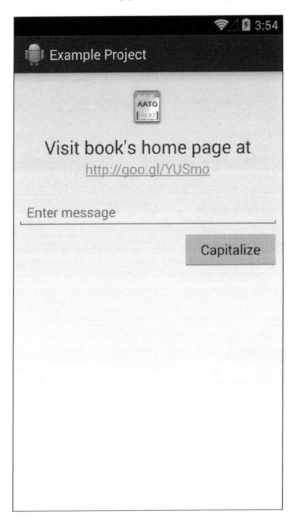

When reading the explanation of the tests in this chapter, at any point, you can refer to the demo application that is provided in order to see the test in action. The previous simple application has a clickable link, text input, click on a button and a defined layout UI, we can test these one by one.

Assertions in depth

Assertions are methods that check for a condition that can be evaluated. If the condition is not met, the assertion method will throw an exception, thereby aborting the execution of the test.

The JUnit API includes the class `Assert`. This is the base class of all the `TestCase` classes that hold several assertion methods useful for writing tests. These inherited methods test for a variety of conditions and are overloaded to support different parameter types. They can be grouped together in the following different sets, depending on the condition checked, for example:

- assertEquals
- assertTrue
- assertFalse
- assertNull
- assertNotNull
- assertSame
- assertNotSame
- fail

The condition tested is pretty obvious and is easily identifiable by the method name. Perhaps the ones that deserve some attention are `assertEquals()` and `assertSame()`. The former, when used on objects, asserts that both objects passed as parameters are equally calling the objects' `equals()` method. The latter asserts that both objects refer to the same object. If, in some case, `equals()` is not implemented by the class, then `assertEquals()` and `assertSame()` will do the same thing.

When one of these assertions fails inside a test, an `AssertionFailedException` is thrown, and this indicates that the test has failed.

Occasionally, during the development process, you might need to create a test that you are not implementing at that precise time. However, you want to flag that the creation of the test was postponed (we did this in *Chapter 1, Getting Started with Testing*, when we added just the test method stubs). In such cases, you can use the `fail()` method, which always fails and uses a custom message that indicates the condition:

```
public void testNotImplementedYet() {
  fail("Not implemented yet");
}
```

Still, there is another common use for `fail()` that is worth mentioning. If we need to test whether a method throws an exception, we can surround the code with a try-catch block and force a fail if the exception was not thrown. For example:

```java
public void testShouldThrowException() {
    try {
        MyFirstProjectActivity.methodThatShouldThrowException();
        fail("Exception was not thrown");
    } catch ( Exception ex ) {
        // do nothing
    }
}
```

 JUnit4 has the annotation `@Test (expected=Exception.class)`, and this supersedes the need for using `fail()` when testing exceptions. With this annotation, the test will only pass if the expected exception is thrown.

Custom messages

It is worth knowing that all `assert` methods provide an overloaded version including a custom `String` message. Should the assertion fail, this custom message will be printed by the test runner, instead of a default message.

The premise behind this is that, sometimes, the generic error message does not reveal enough details, and it is not obvious how the test failed. This custom message can be extremely useful to easily identify the failure once you are looking at the test report, so it's highly recommended as a best practice to use this version.

The following is an example of a simple test that uses this recommendation:

```java
public void testMax() {
int a = 10;
int b = 20;

int actual = Math.max(a, b);

String failMsg = "Expected: " + b + " but was: " + actual;
assertEquals(failMsg, b, actual);
}
```

In the preceding example, we can see another practice that would help you organize and understand your tests easily. This is the use of explicit names for variables that hold the actual values.

 There are other libraries available that have better default error messages and also a more fluid interface for testing. One of these that is worth looking at is Fest (`https://code.google.com/p/fest/`).

Static imports

Though basic assertion methods are inherited from the Assert base class, some other assertions need specific imports. To improve the readability of your tests, there is a pattern to statically import the assert methods from the corresponding classes. Using this pattern instead of having:

```
public void testAlignment() {
int margin = 0;
  ...
 android.test.ViewAsserts.assertRightAligned(errorMsg, editText,
margin);
  }
```

We can simplify it by adding the static import:

```
import static android.test.ViewAsserts.assertRightAligned;
```

```
public void testAlignment() {
    int margin = 0;
    assertRightAligned(errorMsg, editText, margin);
}
```

View assertions

The assertions introduced earlier handle a variety of types as parameters, but they are only intended to test simple conditions or simple objects.

For example, we have `asertEquals(short expected, short actual)` to test short values, `assertEquals(int expected, int actual)` to test integer values, `assertEquals(Object expected, Object expected)` to test any `Object` instance, and so on.

Usually, while testing user interfaces in Android, you will face the problem of more sophisticated methods, which are mainly related with Views. In this respect, Android provides a class with plenty of assertions in `android.test.ViewAsserts` (see `http://developer.android.com/reference/android/test/ViewAsserts.html` for more details), which test relationships between Views and their absolute and relative positions on the screen.

These methods are also overloaded to provide different conditions. Among the assertions, we can find the following:

- `assertBaselineAligned`: This asserts that two Views are aligned on their baseline; that is, their baselines are on the same y location.

- `assertBottomAligned`: This asserts that two views are bottom aligned; that is, their bottom edges are on the same y location.

- `assertGroupContains`: This asserts that the specified group contains a specific child once and only once.

- `assertGroupIntegrity`: This asserts the specified group's integrity. The child count should be >= 0 and each child should be non-null.

- `assertGroupNotContains`: This asserts that the specified group does not contain a specific child.

- `assertHasScreenCoordinates`: This asserts that a View has a particular x and y position on the visible screen.

- `assertHorizontalCenterAligned`: This asserts that the test View is horizontally center aligned with respect to the reference view.

- `assertLeftAligned`: This asserts that two Views are left aligned; that is, their left edges are on the same x location. An optional margin can also be provided.

- `assertOffScreenAbove`: This asserts that the specified view is above the visible screen.

- `assertOffScreenBelow`: This asserts that the specified view is below the visible screen.

- `assertOnScreen`: This asserts that a View is on the screen.

- `assertRightAligned`: This asserts that two Views are right-aligned; that is, their right edges are on the same x location. An optional margin can also be specified.

- assertTopAligned: This asserts that two Views are top aligned; that is, their top edges are on the same y location. An optional margin can also be specified.

- assertVerticalCenterAligned: This asserts that the test View is vertically center-aligned with respect to the reference View.

The following example shows how you can use ViewAssertions to test the user interface layout:

```
public void testUserInterfaceLayout() {
    int margin = 0;
    View origin = mActivity.getWindow().getDecorView();
    assertOnScreen(origin, editText);
    assertOnScreen(origin, button);
    assertRightAligned(editText, button, margin);
}
```

The assertOnScreen method uses an origin to start looking for the requested Views. In this case, we are using the top-level window decor View. If, for some reason, you don't need to go that high in the hierarchy, or if this approach is not suitable for your test, you may use another root View in the hierarchy, for example View.getRootView(), which, in our concrete example, would be editText. getRootView().

Even more assertions

If the assertions that are reviewed previously do not seem to be enough for your tests' needs, there is still another class included in the Android framework that covers other cases. This class is MoreAsserts (http://developer.android.com/reference/android/test/MoreAsserts.html).

These methods are also overloaded to support different parameter types. Among the assertions, we can find the following:

- assertAssignableFrom: This asserts that an object is assignable to a class.

- assertContainsRegex: This asserts that an expected Regex matches any substring of the specified String. It fails with the specified message if it does not.

- assertContainsInAnyOrder: This asserts that the specified Iterable contains precisely the elements expected, but in any order.

- assertContainsInOrder: This asserts that the specified Iterable contains precisely the elements expected, but in the same order.

- assertEmpty: This asserts that an Iterable is empty.

- assertEquals: This is for some Collections not covered in JUnit asserts.

- assertMatchesRegex: This asserts that the specified Regex exactly matches the String and fails with the provided message if it does not.

- assertNotContainsRegex: This asserts that the specified Regex does not match any substring of the specified String, and fails with the provided message if it does.

- assertNotEmpty: This asserts that some Collections not covered in JUnit asserts are not empty.

- assertNotMatchesRegex: This asserts that the specified Regex does not exactly match the specified String, and fails with the provided message if it does.

- checkEqualsAndHashCodeMethods: This is a utility used to test the equals() and hashCode() results at once. This tests whether equals() that is applied to both objects matches the specified result.

The following test checks for an error during the invocation of the capitalization method called via a click on the UI button:

```
@UiThreadTest
public void testNoErrorInCapitalization() {
String msg = "capitalize this text";
editText.setText(msg);

button.performClick();

String actual = editText.getText().toString();
String notExpectedRegexp = "(?i:ERROR)";
String errorMsg = "Capitalization error for " + actual;
assertNotContainsRegex(errorMsg, notExpectedRegexp, actual);
}
```

If you are not familiar with regular expressions, invest some time and visit http://developer.android.com/reference/java/util/regex/package-summary.html because it will be worth it!

In this particular case, we are looking for the word ERROR contained in the result with a case-insensitive match (setting the flag i for this purpose). That is, if for some reason, capitalization doesn't work in our application, and it contains an error message, we can detect this condition with the assertion.

Note that because this is a test that modifies the user interface, we must annotate it with @UiThreadTest; otherwise, it won't be able to alter the UI from a different thread, and we will receive the following exception:

```
INFO/TestRunner(610): ----- begin exception -----
INFO/TestRunner(610): android.view.ViewRoot$CalledFromWro
ngThreadException: Only the original thread that created
a view hierarchy can touch its views.
INFO/TestRunner(610):     at android.view.ViewRoot.
checkThread(ViewRoot.java:2932)
[...]
INFO/TestRunner(610):     at android.app.Instrumentation$
InstrumentationThread.run(Instrumentation.java:1447)
INFO/TestRunner(610): ----- end exception -----
```

The TouchUtils class

Sometimes, when testing UIs, it is helpful to simulate different kinds of touch events. These touch events can be generated in many different ways, but probably android. test.TouchUtils is the simplest to use. This class provides reusable methods to generate touch events in test cases that are derived from InstrumentationTestCase.

The featured methods allow a simulated interaction with the UI under test. The TouchUtils class provides the infrastructure to inject the events using the correct UI or main thread, so no special handling is needed, and you don't need to annotate the test using @UIThreadTest.

TouchUtils supports the following:

- Clicking on a View and releasing it
- Tapping on a View (touching it and quickly releasing)
- Long-clicking on a View
- Dragging the screen
- Dragging Views

The following test represents a typical usage of TouchUtils:

```
public void testListScrolling() {
    listView.scrollTo(0, 0);

    TouchUtils.dragQuarterScreenUp(this, activity);
```

```
        int actualItemPosition = listView.getFirstVisiblePosition();

        assertTrue("Wrong position", actualItemPosition > 0);
    }
```

This test does the following:

- Repositions the list at the beginning to start from a known condition
- Scrolls the list
- Checks for the first visible position to see that it was correctly scrolled

Even the most complex UIs can be tested in that way, and it would help you detect a variety of conditions that could potentially affect the user experience.

Mock objects

We have seen the mock objects provided by the Android testing framework in *Chapter 1, Getting Started with Testing*, and evaluated the concerns about not using real objects to isolate our tests from the surrounding environment.

The next chapter deals with Test-driven Development, and if we were Test-driven Development purists, we can argue about the use of mock objects and be more inclined to use real ones. Martin Fowler calls these two styles the *classical* and *mockist* Test-driven Development dichotomy in his great article *Mocks aren't stubs*, which can be read online at `http://www.martinfowler.com/articles/mocksArentStubs.html`.

Independent of this discussion, we are introducing mock objects as one of the available building blocks because, sometimes, using mock objects in our tests is recommended, desirable, useful, or even unavoidable.

The Android SDK provides the following classes in the subpackage `android.test. mock` to help us:

- `MockApplication`: This is a mock implementation of the `Application` class. All methods are non-functional and throw `UnsupportedOperationException`.
- `MockContentProvider`: This is a mock implementation of `ContentProvider`. All methods are non-functional and throw `UnsupportedOperationException`.
- `MockContentResolver`: This is a mock implementation of the `ContentResolver` class that isolates the test code from the real content system. All methods are non-functional and throw `UnsupportedOperationException`.

- `MockContext`: This is a mock context class, and this can be used to inject other dependencies. All methods are non-functional and throw `UnsupportedOperationException`.

- `MockCursor`: This is a mock Cursor class that isolates the test code from real Cursor implementation. All methods are non-functional and throw `UnsupportedOperationException`.

- `MockDialogInterface`: This is a mock implementation of the `DialogInterface` class. All methods are non-functional and throw `UnsupportedOperationException`.

- `MockPackageManager`: This is a mock implementation of the `PackageManager` class. All methods are non-functional and throw `UnsupportedOperationException`.

- `MockResources`: This is a mock `Resources` class.

All of these classes have non-functional methods that throw `UnsupportedOperationException` when used. If you need to use some of these methods, or if you detect that your test is failing with this `Exception`, you should extend one of these base classes and provide the required functionality.

An overview of MockContext

This mock can be used to inject other dependencies, mocks, or monitors into the classes under test. Extend this class to provide your desired behavior, overriding the correspondent methods. The Android SDK provides some prebuilt mock `Context` objects, each of which has a separate use case.

The IsolatedContext class

In your tests, you might find the need to isolate the Activity under test from other Android components to prevent unwanted interactions. This can be a complete isolation, but sometimes, this isolation avoids interacting with other components, and for your Activity to still run correctly, some connection with the system is required.

For those cases, the Android SDK provides `android.test.IsolatedContext`, a mock `Context` that not only prevents interaction with most of the underlying system but also satisfies the needs of interacting with other packages or components such as `Services` or `ContentProviders`.

Alternate route to file and database operations

In some cases, all we need is to be able to provide an alternate route to the file and database operations. For example, if we are testing the application on a real device, we perhaps don't want to affect the existing database but use our own testing data.

Such cases can take advantage of another class that is not part of the `android.test.mock` subpackage but is part of `android.test` instead, that is, `RenamingDelegatingContext`.

This class lets us alter operations on files and databases by having a prefix that is specified in the constructor. All other operations are delegated to the delegating Context that you must specify in the constructor too.

Suppose our `Activity` under test uses a database we want to control, probably introducing specialized content or fixture data to drive our tests, and we don't want to use the real files. In this case, we create a `RenamingDelegatingContext` class that specifies a prefix, and our unchanged Activity will use this prefix to create any files.

For example, if our Activity tries to access a file named `birthdays.txt`, and we provide a `RenamingDelegatingContext` class that specifies the prefix `test`, then this same Activity will access the file `testbirthdays.txt` instead when it is being tested.

The MockContentResolver class

The `MockContentResolver` class implements all methods in a non-functional way and throws the exception `UnsupportedOperationException` if you attempt to use them. The reason for this class is to isolate tests from the real content.

Let's say your application uses a `ContentProvider` class to feed your Activity information. You can create unit tests for this `ContentProvider` using `ProviderTestCase2`, which we will be analyzing shortly, but when we try to produce functional or integration tests for the Activity against `ContentProvider`, it's not so evident as to what test case to use. The most obvious choice is `ActivityInstrumentationTestCase2`, mainly if your functional tests simulate user experience because you might need the `sendKeys()` method or similar methods, which are readily available on these tests.

The first problem you might encounter then is that it's unclear as to where to inject a `MockContentResolver` in your test to be able to use test data with your `ContentProvider`. There's no way to inject a `MockContext` either.

This problem will be solved in *Chapter 3, Baking with Testing Recipes* where further details are provided.

The TestCase base class

This is the base class of all other test cases in the JUnit framework. It implements the basic methods that we were analyzing in the previous examples (`setUp()`). The `TestCase` class also implements the `junit.framework.Test` interface, meaning it can be run as a JUnit test.

Your Android test cases should always extend `TestCase` or one of its descendants.

The default constructor

All test cases require a default constructor because, sometimes, depending on the test runner used, this is the only constructor that is invoked, and is also used for serialization.

According to the documentation, this method is not intended to be used by "mere mortals" without calling `setName(String name)`.

Therefore, to appease the Gods, a common pattern is to use a default test case name in this constructor and invoke the `given name` constructor afterwards:

```
public class MyTestCase extends TestCase {
    public MyTestCase() {
        this("MyTestCase Default Name");
    }

    public MyTestCase(String name) {
        super(name);
    }
}
```

Downloading the example code

You can download the example code files from your account at `http://www.packtpub.com` for all the Packt Publishing books you have purchased. If you purchased this book elsewhere, you can visit `http://www.packtpub.com/support` and register to have the files e-mailed directly to you.

The given name constructor

This constructor takes a name as an argument to label the test case. It will appear in test reports and would be of much help when you try to identify where failed tests have come from.

The setName() method

There are some classes that extend `TestCase` that don't provide a given name constructor. In such cases, the only alternative is to call `setName(String name)`.

The AndroidTestCase base class

This class can be used as a base class for general-purpose Android test cases.

Use it when you need access to Android resources, databases, or files in the filesystem. Context is stored as a field in this class, which is conveniently named `mContext` and can be used inside the tests if needed, or the `getContext()` method can be used too.

Tests based on this class can start more than one Activity using `Context.startActivity()`.

There are various test cases in Android SDK that extend this base class:

- `ApplicationTestCase<T extends Application>`
- `ProviderTestCase2<T extends ContentProvider>`
- `ServiceTestCase<T extends Service>`

When using the `AndroidTestCase` Java class, you inherit some base assertion methods that can be used; let's look at these in more detail.

The assertActivityRequiresPermission() method

The signature for this method is as follows:

```
public void assertActivityRequiresPermission(String packageName,
String className, String permission)
```

Description

This assertion method checks whether the launching of a particular Activity is protected by a specific permission. It takes the following three parameters:

- `packageName`: This is a string that indicates the package name of the activity to launch

- `className`: This is a string that indicates the class of the activity to launch

- `permission`: This is a string with the permission to check

The Activity is launched and then `SecurityException` is expected, which mentions that the required permission is missing in the error message. The actual instantiation of an activity is not handled by this assertion, and thus, an Instrumentation is not needed.

Example

This test checks the requirement of the `android.Manifest.permission.WRITE_EXTERNAL_STORAGE` permission, which is needed to write to external storage, in the `MyContactsActivity` Activity:

```
public void testActivityPermission() {
    String pkg = "com.blundell.tut";
    String activity =  PKG + ".MyContactsActivity";
    String permission = android.Manifest.permission.CALL_PHONE;
    assertActivityRequiresPermission(pkg, activity, permission);
}
```

Always use the constants that describe the permissions from `android.Manifest.permission`, not the strings, so if the implementation changes, your code will still be valid.

The assertReadingContentUriRequiresPermission method

The signature for this method is as follows:

```
public void assertReadingContentUriRequiresPermission(Uri uri, String permission)
```

Description

This assertion method checks whether reading from a specific URI requires the permission provided as a parameter.

It takes the following two parameters:

- `uri`: This is the Uri that requires a permission to query
- `permission`: This is a string that contains the permission to query

If a `SecurityException` class is generated, which contains the specified permission, this assertion is validated.

Example

This test tries to read contacts and verifies that the correct `SecurityException` is generated:

```
public void testReadingContacts() {
   Uri URI = ContactsContract.AUTHORITY_URI;
   String PERMISSION = android.Manifest.permission.READ_CONTACTS;
   assertReadingContentUriRequiresPermission(URI, PERMISSION);
}
```

The assertWritingContentUriRequiresPermission() method

The signature for this method is as follows:

```
public void assertWritingContentUriRequiresPermission (Uri uri,
   String permission)
```

Description

This assertion method checks whether inserting into a specific `Uri` requires the permission provided as a parameter.

It takes the following two parameters:

- `uri`: This is the Uri that requires a permission to query
- `permission`: This is a string that contains the permission to query

If a `SecurityException` class is generated, which contains the specified permission, this assertion is validated.

Example

This test tries to write to Contacts and verifies that the correct `SecurityException` is generated:

```
public void testWritingContacts() {
Uri uri = ContactsContract.AUTHORITY_URI;
 String permission = android.Manifest.permission.WRITE_CONTACTS;
 assertWritingContentUriRequiresPermission(uri, permission);
}
```

Instrumentation

Instrumentation is instantiated by the system before any of the application code is run, thereby allowing monitoring of all the interactions between the system and the application.

As with many other Android application components, instrumentation implementations are described in the `AndroidManifest.xml` under the tag `<instrumentation>`. However, with the advent of Gradle, this has now been automated for us, and we can change the properties of the instrumentation in the app's `build.gradle` file. The `AndroidManifest` file for your tests will be automatically generated:

```
defaultConfig {
   testApplicationId 'com.blundell.tut.tests'
testInstrumentationRunner
   "android.test.InstrumentationTestRunner"
}
```

The values mentioned in the preceding code are also the defaults if you do not declare them, meaning that you don't have to have any of these parameters to start writing tests.

The `testApplicationId` attribute defines the name of the package for your tests. As a default, it is your application under the test package name + `tests`. You can declare a custom test runner using `testInstrumentationRunner`. This is handy if you want to have tests run in a custom way, for example, parallel test execution.

There are also many other parameters in development, and I would advise you to keep your eyes upon the Google Gradle plugin website (`http://tools.android.com/tech-docs/new-build-system/user-guide`).

The ActivityMonitor inner class

As mentioned earlier, the Instrumentation class is used to monitor the interaction between the system and the application or the Activities under test. The inner class Instrumentation `ActivityMonitor` allows the monitoring of a single Activity within an application.

Example

Let's pretend that we have a TextView in our Activity that holds a URL and has its auto link property set:

```
<TextView
    android:id="@+id/link"
    android:layout_width="match_parent"
    android:layout_height="wrap_content"
    android:text="@string/home"
    android:autoLink="web" " />
```

If we want to verify that, when clicked, the hyperlink is correctly followed and some browser is invoked, we can create a test like this:

```
public void testFollowLink() {
    IntentFilter intentFilter = new IntentFilter(Intent.ACTION_
VIEW);
    intentFilter.addDataScheme("http");
    intentFilter.addCategory(Intent.CATEGORY_BROWSABLE);

    Instrumentation inst = getInstrumentation();
    ActivityMonitor monitor = inst.addMonitor(intentFilter, null,
false);
    TouchUtils.clickView(this, linkTextView);
```

```
        monitor.waitForActivityWithTimeout(3000);
        int monitorHits = monitor.getHits();
        inst.removeMonitor(monitor);

        assertEquals(1, monitorHits);
    }
```

Here, we will do the following:

1. Create an IntentFilter for intents that would open a browser.
2. Add a monitor to our Instrumentation based on the `IntentFilter` class.
3. Click on the hyperlink.
4. Wait for the activity (hopefully the browser).
5. Verify that the monitor hits were incremented.
6. Remove the monitor.

Using monitors, we can test even the most complex interactions with the system and other Activities. This is a very powerful tool to create integration tests.

The InstrumentationTestCase class

The `InstrumentationTestCase` class is the direct or indirect base class for various test cases that have access to Instrumentation. This is the list of the most important direct and indirect subclasses:

- `ActivityTestCase`
- `ProviderTestCase2<T extends ContentProvider>`
- `SingleLaunchActivityTestCase<T extends Activity>`
- `SyncBaseInstrumentation`
- `ActivityInstrumentationTestCase2<T extends Activity>`
- `ActivityUnitTestCase<T extends Activity>`

The `InstrumentationTestCase` class is in the `android.test` package, and extends `junit.framework.TestCase`, which extends `junit.framework.Assert`.

The launchActivity and launchActivityWithIntent methods

These utility methods are used to launch Activities from a test. If the Intent is not specified using the second option, a default Intent is used:

```
public final T launchActivity (String pkg, Class<T> activityCls,
    Bundle extras)
```

 The template class parameter T is used in activityCls and as the return type, limiting its use to Activities of that type.

If you need to specify a custom Intent, you can use the following code that also adds the intent parameter:

```
public final T launchActivityWithIntent (String pkg, Class<T>
    activityCls, Intent intent)
```

The sendKeys and sendRepeatedKeys methods

While testing Activities' UI, you will face the need to simulate interaction with qwerty-based keyboards or DPAD buttons to send keys to complete fields, select shortcuts, or navigate throughout the different components.

This is what the different sendKeys and sendRepeatedKeys are used for.

There is one version of sendKeys that accepts integer keys values. They can be obtained from constants defined in the KeyEvent class.

For example, we can use the sendKeys method in this way:

```
public void testSendKeyInts() {
    requestMessageInputFocus();
    sendKeys(
            KeyEvent.KEYCODE_H,
            KeyEvent.KEYCODE_E,
            KeyEvent.KEYCODE_E,
            KeyEvent.KEYCODE_E,
            KeyEvent.KEYCODE_Y,
            KeyEvent.KEYCODE_DPAD_DOWN,
```

```
                    KeyEvent.KEYCODE_ENTER);
        String actual = messageInput.getText().toString();

            assertEquals("HEEEY", actual);
    }
```

Here, we are sending H, E, and Y letter keys and then the ENTER key using their integer representations to the Activity under test.

Alternatively, we can create a string by concatenating the keys we desire to send, discarding the KEYCODE prefix, and separating them with spaces that are ultimately ignored:

```
        public void testSendKeyString() {
            requestMessageInputFocus();

            sendKeys("H 3*E Y DPAD_DOWN ENTER");
            String actual = messageInput.getText().toString();

            assertEquals("HEEEY", actual);
        }
```

Here, we did exactly the same as in the previous test but we used a String "H 3* EY DPAD_DOWN ENTER". Note that every key in the String can be prefixed by a repeating factor followed by * and the key to be repeated. We used 3*E in our previous example, which is the same as E E E, that is, three times the letter E.

If sending repeated keys is what we need in our tests, there is also another alternative that is precisely intended for these cases:

```
    public void testSendRepeatedKeys() {
        requestMessageInputFocus();

        sendRepeatedKeys(
                1, KeyEvent.KEYCODE_H,
                3, KeyEvent.KEYCODE_E,
                1, KeyEvent.KEYCODE_Y,
                1, KeyEvent.KEYCODE_DPAD_DOWN,
                1, KeyEvent.KEYCODE_ENTER);
        String actual = messageInput.getText().toString();

        assertEquals("HEEEY", actual);
    }
```

This is the same test implemented in a different manner. The repetition number precedes each key.

The runTestOnUiThread helper method

The `runTestOnUiThread` method is a helper method used to run portions of a test on the UI thread. We used this inside the method `requestMessageInputFocus()`; so that we can set the focus on our EditText before waiting for the application to be idle, using `Instrumentation.waitForIdleSync()`. Also, the `runTestOnUiThread` method throws an exception, so we have to deal with this case:

```
private void requestMessageInputFocus() {
        try {
            runTestOnUiThread(new Runnable() {
                @Override
                public void run() {
                    messageInput.requestFocus();
                }
            });
        } catch (Throwable throwable) {
            fail("Could not request focus.");
        }
        instrumentation.waitForIdleSync();
    }
```

Alternatively, as we have discussed before, to run a test on the UI thread, we can annotate it with `@UiThreadTest`. However, sometimes, we need to run only parts of the test on the UI thread because other parts of it are not suitable to run on that thread, for example, database calls, or we are using other helper methods that provide the infrastructure themselves to use the UI thread, for example the `TouchUtils` methods.

The ActivityTestCase class

This is mainly a class that holds common code for other test cases that access Instrumentation.

You can use this class if you are implementing a specific behavior for test cases and the existing alternatives don't fit your requirements. This means you are unlikely to use this class unless you want to implement a new base class for other tests to use. For example, consider a scenario where Google brings out a new component and you want to write tests around it (like `SuperNewContentProvider`).

If this is not the case, you might find the following options more suitable for your requirements:

- `ActivityInstrumentationTestCase2<T extends Activity>`
- `ActivityUnitTestCase<T extends Activity>`

The abstract class `android.test.ActivityTestCase` extends `android.test.InstrumentationTestCase` and serves as a base class for other different test cases, such as `android.test.ActivityInstrumentationTestCase`, `android.test.ActivityInstrumentationTestCase2`, and `android.test.ActivityUnitTestCase`.

 The `android.test.ActivityInstrumentationTestCase` test case is a deprecated class since Android API Level 3 (Android 1.5) and should not be used in newer projects. Even though it was deprecated long ago, it has a great name for auto import, so be careful!

The scrubClass method

The `scrubClass` method is one of the protected methods in the class:

```
protected void scrubClass(Class<?> testCaseClass)
```

It is invoked from the `tearDown()` method in several of the discussed test case implementations in order to clean up class variables that may have been instantiated as non-static inner classes so as to avoid holding references to them.

This is in order to prevent memory leaks for large test suites.

`IllegalAccessException` is thrown if a problem is encountered while accessing these class variables.

The ActivityInstrumentationTestCase2 class

The `ActivityInstrumentationTestCase2` class would probably be the one you use the most to write functional Android test cases. It provides functional testing of a single Activity.

This class has access to Instrumentation and will create the Activity under test using the system infrastructure, by calling `InstrumentationTestCase.launchActivity()`. The Activity can then be manipulated and monitored after creation.

If you need to provide a custom Intent to start your Activity, before invoking `getActivity()`, you may inject an Intent with `setActivityIntent(Intent intent)`.

This test case would be very useful to test interactions through the user interface as events can be injected to simulate user behavior.

The constructor

There is only one public non-deprecated constructor for this class, which is as follows:

```
ActivityInstrumentationTestCase2(Class<T> activityClass)
```

It should be invoked with an instance of the `Activity` class for the same Activity used as a class template parameter.

The setUp method

The `setUp` method is the precise place to initialize the test case fields and other fixture components that require initialization.

This is an example that shows some of the patterns that you might repeatedly find in your test cases:

```
@Override
protected void setUp() throws Exception {
  super.setUp();
  // this must be called before getActivity()
  // disabling touch mode allows for sending key events
  setActivityInitialTouchMode(false);

  activity = getActivity();
```

```
    instrumentation = getInstrumentation();
    linkTextView = (TextView) activity.findViewById(R.id.main_text_
link);
    messageInput = (EditText) activity.findViewById(R.id.main_input_
message);
    capitalizeButton = (Button) activity.findViewById(R.id.main_button_
capitalize);
  }
```

We perform the following actions:

1. Invoke the super method. This is a JUnit pattern that should be followed here to ensure correct operation.

2. Disable the touch mode. To take effect, this should be done before the Activity is created, by invoking `getActivity()`. It sets the initial touch mode of the Activity under test as disabled. The touch mode is a fundamental Android UI concept, and is discussed in `http://developer.android.com/guide/topics/ui/ui-events.html#TouchMode`.

3. Start the Activity using `getActivity()`.

4. Get the instrumentation. We have access to the instrumentation because `ActivityInstrumentationTestCase2` extends `InstrumentationTestCase`.

5. Find the Views and set the fields. In these operations, note that the `R` class used is from the target package and not from the tests.

The tearDown method

Usually, this method cleans up what was initialized in `setUp`. For instance, if you were creating an integration test that sets up a mock web server before your tests, you would want to tear it back down afterwards to free up resources.

In this example, we ensure that the object we used is disposed of:

```
@Override
protected void tearDown() throws Exception {
    super.tearDown();
      myObject.dispose();
}
```

The ProviderTestCase2<T> class

This is a test case designed to test the ContentProvider classes.

The ProviderTestCase2 class also extends AndroidTestCase. The class template parameter T represents ContentProvider under test. Implementation of this test uses IsolatedContext and MockContentResolver, which are mock objects that we described before in this chapter.

The constructor

There is only one public non-deprecated constructor for this class. This is as follows:

```
ProviderTestCase2(Class<T> providerClass, String
    providerAuthority)
```

This should be invoked with an instance of the ContentProvider class for the same ContentProvider class used as a class template parameter.

The second parameter is the authority for the provider, which is usually defined as the AUTHORITY constant in the ContentProvider class.

An example

This is a typical example of a ContentProvider test:

```
public void testQuery() {
    String segment = "dummySegment";
    Uri uri = Uri.withAppendedPath(MyProvider.CONTENT_URI, segment);
    Cursor c = provider.query(uri, null, null, null, null);
    try {
      int actual = c.getCount();

        assertEquals(2, actual);
    } finally {
        c.close();
    }
}
```

In this test, we are expecting the query to return a Cursor that contains two rows (this is just an example that uses the number of rows that applies for your particular case) and asserts this condition.

Usually, in the setUp method, we obtain a reference to the mProvider provider in this example, using getProvider().

What is interesting to note is that because these tests are using
`MockContentResolver` and `IsolatedContext`, the content of the real database is not
affected, and we can also run destructive tests like this one:

```
public void testDeleteByIdDeletesCorrectNumberOfRows() {
    String segment = "dummySegment";
    Uri uri = Uri.withAppendedPath(MyProvider.CONTENT_URI, segment);

    int actual = provider.delete(uri, "_id = ?", new String[]{"1"});

    assertEquals(1, actual);
}
```

This test deletes some content from the database, but the database is restored to its
initial content afterwards not to affect other tests.

The ServiceTestCase<T>

This is a test case specially created to test services. The methods to exercise the
service life cycle, such as `setupService`, `startService`, `bindService`, and
`shutDownService`, are also included in this class.

The constructor

There is only one public non-deprecated constructor for this class. This is as follows:

```
ServiceTestCase(Class<T> serviceClass)
```

It should be invoked with an instance of the `Service` class for the same `Service`
used as a class template parameter.

The TestSuiteBuilder.FailedToCreateTests class

The `TestSuiteBuilder.FailedToCreateTests` class is a special `TestCase` class
used to indicate a failure during the `build()` step. That is, during the test suite
creation, if an error is detected, you will receive an exception like this one, which
indicates the failure to construct the test suite:

```
INFO/TestRunner(1): java.lang.RuntimeException: Exception during suite
construction
```

```
INFO/TestRunner(1):      at android.test.suitebuilder.TestSuiteBuilder$Fai
ledToCreateTests.testSuiteConstructionFailed(TestSuiteBuilder.java:239)

INFO/TestRunner(1):      at java.lang.reflect.Method.invokeNative(Native
Method)

[...]

INFO/TestRunner(1):      at android.test.InstrumentationTestRunner.onStart
(InstrumentationTestRunner.java:520)

INFO/TestRunner(1):      at android.app.Instrumentation$InstrumentationThr
ead.run(Instrumentation.java:1447)
```

Using libraries in test projects

Your Android project might require an external Java library or an Android library.
Now, we will explain how to incorporate these in your project that is ready to
be tested. Note that the following explains the usage of a local module that is an
Android library, but the same rules can be applied to an external JAR (Java library)
file or an external AAR (Android library) file.

Let's pretend that in one Activity, we are creating objects from a class that is part of a
library. For the sake of our example, let's say the library is called dummyLibrary, and
the mentioned class is Dummy.

So our Activity would look like this:

```java
import com.blundell.dummylibrary.Dummy;

public class MyFirstProjectActivity extends Activity {
    private Dummy dummy;

    @Override
    public void onCreate(Bundle savedInstanceState) {
        super.onCreate(savedInstanceState);
        setContentView(R.layout.activity_main);

        final EditText messageInput = (EditText) findViewById(R.
id.main_input_message);
        Button capitalizeButton = (Button) findViewById(R.id.main_
button_capitalize);
        capitalizeButton.setOnClickListener(new OnClickListener() {
            @Override
            public void onClick(View v) {
                String input = messageInput.getText().toString();
                messageInput.setText(input.toUpperCase());
```

```
            }
        });

        dummy = new Dummy();
    }

    public Dummy getDummy() {
        return dummy;
    }

    public static void methodThatShouldThrowException() throws
Exception {
        throw new Exception("This is an exception");
    }

}
```

This library is an Android AAR module, and so it should be added to your `build.gradle` dependencies in the normal way:

```
dependencies {
    compile project(':dummylibrary')
}
```

If this was an external library, you would replace `project(':dummylibrary')` with `'com.external.lib:name:version'`.

Now, let's create a simple test. From our previous experience, we know that if we need to test an Activity, we should use `ActivityInstrumentationTestCase2`, and this is precisely what we will do. Our simple test will be as follows:

```
public void testDummy() {
    assertNotNull(activity.getDummy());
}
```

The test in the preceding code runs and passes in the first instance! Note that in the not-so-distant past (pre-Gradle), the test would not have even compiled. We would have had to jump through hoops, adding the test library to our Android tests project, or making the JAR/AAR file exportable from our main project. It's a nice time to stop and reflect on the power of Gradle and Android Studio that give us a lot of manual setup for free.

Summary

We investigated the most relevant building blocks and reusable patterns to create our tests. Along this journey, we:

- Understood the common assertions found in JUnit tests
- Explained the specialized assertions found in the Android SDK
- Explored Android mock objects and their use in Android tests
- Exemplified the use of the different test cases available in the Android SDK

Now that we have all the building blocks, it is time to start creating more and more tests to acquire the experience needed to master the technique.

The next chapter will provide you with examples of when and where to use different test cases on Android. This will give us a great breadth of expertise in knowing what testing methodology to apply when we have a specific scenario to test.

3
Baking with Testing Recipes

This chapter provides practical examples of multiple common situations that you will encounter, by applying the disciplines and techniques described in the previous chapters. The examples are presented in an easy-to-follow manner, so you can adapt and use them for your own projects.

The following are the topics that will be covered in this chapter:

- Android unit tests
- Testing activities and applications
- Testing databases and content providers
- Testing local and remote services
- Testing user interfaces
- Testing exceptions
- Testing parsers
- Testing for memory leaks
- Testing with Espresso

After this chapter, you will have a reference to apply different testing recipes to your projects for different situations.

Android unit tests

There are some cases where you really need to test parts of the application in isolation with little connection to the underlying system. In Android, the system is the Activity framework. In such cases, we have to select a base class that is high enough in the test hierarchy to remove some of the dependencies but not high enough for us to be responsible for some of the basic infrastructure of instantiating Context, for example.

In such cases, the candidate base class is `AndroidTestCase` because this allows the use of Context and Resources without thinking about Activities:

```
public class AccessPrivateDataTest extends AndroidTestCase {
    public void testAccessAnotherAppsPrivateDataIsNotPossible() {
        String filesDirectory = getContext().getFilesDir().getPath();
        String privateFilePath = filesDirectory +
 "/data/com.android.cts.appwithdata/private_file.txt";
        try {
            new FileInputStream(privateFilePath);
            fail("Was able to access another app's private data");
        } catch (FileNotFoundException e) {
            // expected
        }
    }
}
```

 This example is based on the Android **Compatibility Test Suite (CTS)** at `http://source.android.com/compatibility/cts-intro.html`. The CTS is a suite of tests aimed at making the Android hardware and software environment consistent for application developers, irrespective of the original equipment manufacturer.

The `AccessPrivateDataTest` class extends `AndroidTestCase` because it's a unit test that doesn't require the system infrastructure. In this particular case, we could not have used `TestCase` directly because we are using `getContext()` later on.

This test method, `testAccessAnotherAppsPrivateDataIsNotPossible()`, tests the access to another package's private data and fails if access is possible. To achieve this, the expected exceptions are caught, and if this doesn't happen, `fail()` is invoked with a custom message. The test seems pretty straightforward, but you can see how powerful this is to stop inadvertent security mistakes from creeping in.

Testing activities and applications

Here, we cover some common cases that you will find in your day-to-day testing, including dealing with Intents, Preferences, and Context. You can adapt these patterns to suit your specific needs.

Mocking applications and preferences

In Android parlance, an application refers to a base class used when it is needed to maintain a global application state. The full package is `android.app.Application`. This can be utilized when dealing with shared preferences.

We expect that the tests that alter these preferences' values will not affect the behavior of the real application. Without the correct testing framework, the tests could delete user account information for an application that stores these values as shared preferences. This doesn't sound like a good idea. So what we really need is the ability to mock a Context that also mocks the access to `SharedPreferences`.

Our first attempt could be to use `RenamingDelegatingContext`, but unfortunately, it does not mock `SharedPreferences`, although it is close because it mocks the database and filesystem access. So first, we need to mock access to our shared preferences.

 Whenever you come across a new class (like `RenamingDelegatingContext`), it's a good idea to read the relevant Java doc to get an overview of how the framework developers expect it to be used. For more information, refer to `http://developer.android.com/reference/android/test/RenamingDelegatingContext.html`.

The RenamingMockContext class

Let's create the specialized Context. The `RenamingDelegatingContext` class is a very good point to start from because as we mentioned before, database and filesystem access will be mocked. The problem is how to mock the `SharedPreferences` access.

Remember that `RenamingDelegatingContext`, as its name suggests, delegates everything to a Context. So the root of our problem lies in this Context. When you access `SharedPreferences` from a Context, you use `getSharedPreferences(String name, int mode)`. To change the way this method works, we can override it inside `RenamingMockContext`. Now that we have control, we can prepend the name parameter with our test prefix, which means that when our tests run, they will write to a preferences file that is different than that of our main application:

```
public class RenamingMockContext extends RenamingDelegatingContext {

    private static final String PREFIX = "test.";

    public RenamingMockContext(Context context) {
        super(context, PREFIX);
    }

    @Override
    public SharedPreferences getSharedPreferences(String name, int
mode) {
        return super.getSharedPreferences(PREFIX + name, mode);
    }
}
```

Now, we have full control over how preferences, databases, and files are stored.

Mocking contexts

We have the `RenamingMockContext` class. Now, we need a test that uses it. As we will be testing an application, the base class for the test would be `ApplicationTestCase`. This test case provides a framework in which you can test application classes in a controlled environment. It provides basic support for the lifecycle of an application, and hooks to inject various dependencies and control the environment in which your application is tested. Using the `setContext()` method, we can inject the `RenamingMockContext` method before the application is created.

We're going to test an application called `TemperatureConverter`. This is a simple application that converts Celsius to Fahrenheit and vice versa. We will discuss more about the development of this app in *Chapter 6, Practicing Test-driven Development*. For now, the details aren't necessary as we are concentrating on testing scenarios. The `TemperatureConverter` application will store the decimal places of any conversion as a shared preference. Consequently, we will create a test to set the decimal places and then retrieve it to verify its value:

```
public class TemperatureConverterApplicationTests extends ApplicationT
estCase<TemperatureConverterApplication> {

    public TemperatureConverterApplicationTests() {
        this("TemperatureConverterApplicationTests");
    }

    public TemperatureConverterApplicationTests(String name) {
        super(TemperatureConverterApplication.class);
        setName(name);
    }

    public void testSetAndRetreiveDecimalPlaces() {
        RenamingMockContext mockContext = new RenamingMockContext(get
Context());
        setContext(mockContext);
        createApplication();
        TemperatureConverterApplication application =
getApplication();

        application.setDecimalPlaces(3);

        assertEquals(3, application.getDecimalPlaces());
    }
}
```

We extend `ApplicationTestCase` using the `TemperatureConverterApplication` template parameter.

Then, we use the given name constructor pattern that we discussed in *Chapter 2, Understanding Testing with the Android SDK*.

Here, we have not used a `setUp()` method since there is only one test in the class–*you ain't gonna need it* as they say. One day, if you come to add another test to this class, this is when you can override `setUp()` and move the behavior. This follows the DRY principle, meaning Don't Repeat Yourself, and leads to more maintainable software. So at the top of the test method, we create the mock context and set the context for this test using the `setContext()` method; we create the application using `createApplication()`. You need to ensure you call `setContext` before `createApplication` as this is how you get the correct instantiation order. Now, the code that actually tests for the required behavior setting the decimal places, retrieving it, and verifying its value. This is it, using `RenamingMockContext` to give us control over `SharedPreferences`. Whenever the `SharedPreference` is requested, the method will invoke the delegating context, adding the prefix for the name. The original `SharedPreferences` class used by the application are unchanged:

```
public class TemperatureConverterApplication extends Application {
    private static final int DECIMAL_PLACES_DEFAULT = 2;
    private static final String KEY_DECIMAL_PLACES = ".KEY_DECIMAL_
PLACES";

    private SharedPreferences sharedPreferences;

    @Override
    public void onCreate() {
        super.onCreate();
        sharedPreferences = PreferenceManager.getDefaultSharedPrefere
nces(this);
    }

    public void setDecimalPlaces(int places) {
        Editor editor = sharedPreferences.edit();
        editor.putInt(KEY_DECIMAL_PLACES, places);
        editor.apply();
    }

    public int getDecimalPlaces() {
        return sharedPreferences.getInt(KEY_DECIMAL_PLACES, DECIMAL_
PLACES_DEFAULT);
    }
}
```

We can verify that our tests do not affect the application by furnishing the TemperatureConverterApplication class with some value in the shared preferences, running the application, then running the tests and eventually verifying that this value was not affected by executing the tests.

Testing activities

The next example shows how an activity can be tested in complete isolation using the ActivityUnitTestCase<Activity> base class. A second choice would be ActivityInstrumentationTestCase2<Activity>. However, the former allows you to create an Activity but not attach it to the system, meaning you cannot launch other Activities (you are an Activity single unit). This choice of the parent class not only requires more care and attention in your setup but also provides a greater flexibility and control over the Activity under test. This kind of test is intended to test general Activity behavior and not an Activity instance's interaction with other system components or any UI-related tests.

First things first, here is the class under test. It is a simple Activity with one button. When this button is pressed, it fires an Intent to start the Dialer and finishes itself:

```java
public class ForwardingActivity extends Activity {
    private static final int GHOSTBUSTERS = 999121212;
    @Override
    protected void onCreate(Bundle savedInstanceState) {
        super.onCreate(savedInstanceState);
        setContentView(R.layout.activity_forwarding);
        View button = findViewById(R.id.forwarding_go_button);
        button.setOnClickListener(new View.OnClickListener() {
            @Override
            public void onClick(View v) {
                Intent intent = new Intent("tel:" + GHOSTBUSTERS);
                startActivity(intent);
                finish();
            }
        });
    }
}
```

For our test case, we extend ActivityUnitTestCase<ForwardingActivity>, as we mentioned earlier, as a unit test for an Activity class. This activity under test will be disconnected from the system, so it is only intended to test internal aspects of it and not its interaction with other components. In the setUp() method, we create the Intent that will start our Activity under test, that is, ForwardingActivity. Note the use of getInstrumentation(). The getContext class, as at this point in the setUp() method of the Activity Context, is still null:

```
public class ForwardingActivityTest extends ActivityUnitTestCase<Forwa
rdingActivity> {
    private Intent startIntent;

    public ForwardingActivityTest() {
        super(ForwardingActivity.class);
    }

    @Override
    protected void setUp() throws Exception {
        super.setUp();
        Context context = getInstrumentation().getContext();
        startIntent = new Intent(context, ForwardingActivity.class);
    }
```

Now that the setup is done, we can move onto our tests:

```
public void testLaunchingSubActivityFiresIntentAndFinishesSelf() {
Activity activity = startActivity(startIntent, null, null);
View button = activity.findViewById(R.id.forwarding_go_button);

button.performClick();

assertNotNull(getStartedActivityIntent());
assertTrue(isFinishCalled());
}
```

The first test performs a click on the **Go** button of the Forwarding Activity. The onClickListener class of that button invokes startActivity() with an Intent that defines a new Activity that will be started. After performing this action, we verify that the Intent used to launch the new Activity is not null. The getStartedActivityIntent() method returns the Intent that was used if the Activity under tests invoked startActivity(Intent) or startActivityForResult(Intent, int). Next, we assert that finish() was called, and we do that by verifying the return value of FinishCalled(), which returns true if one of the finish methods (finish(), finishFromChild(Activity), or finishActivity(int)) was called in the Activity under test:

```
public void testExampleOfLifeCycleCreation() {
    Activity activity = startActivity(startIntent, null, null);

    // At this point, onCreate() has been called, but nothing else
    // so we complete the startup of the activity
    getInstrumentation().callActivityOnStart(activity);
    getInstrumentation().callActivityOnResume(activity);

    // At this point you could test for various configuration aspects
    // or you could use a Mock Context
    // to confirm that your activity has made
    // certain calls to the system and set itself up properly.

    getInstrumentation().callActivityOnPause(activity);

    // At this point you could confirm that
    // the activity has paused properly,
    // as if it is no longer the topmost activity on screen.

    getInstrumentation().callActivityOnStop(activity);

    // At this point, you could confirm that
    // the activity has shut itself down appropriately,
    // or you could use a Mock Context to confirm that
    // your activity has released any
    // system resources it should no longer be holding.

    // ActivityUnitTestCase.tearDown() is always automatically called
    // and will take care of calling onDestroy().
}
```

The second test is perhaps the more interesting test method in this test case. This test case demonstrates how to exercise the Activity life cycle. After starting the Activity, `onCreate()` is called automatically, and we can then exercise other life cycle methods by invoking them manually. To be able to invoke these methods, we use `Intrumentation` of this test. Also, we don't manually invoke `onDestroy()` as it will be invoked for us in `tearDown()`.

Let's walk through the code. This method starts the Activity in the same way as the previously analyzed test. After the activity is started, its `onCreate()` method is called automatically by the system. We then use `Instrumentation` to invoke other life cycle methods to complete the Activity under test start up. These correspond to `onStart()` and `onResume()` in the Activity life cycle.

The Activity is now completely started, and it's time to test for the aspects we are interested in. Once this is achieved, we can follow other steps in the life cycle. Note that this sample test does not assert anything here but simply points out how to step through the life cycle. To finish the life cycle, we call through to `onPause()` and `onStop()`. As we know, `onDestroy()` is avoided as it will automatically be called by `tearDown()`.

This test represents a test skeleton. You can reuse it to test your Activities in isolation and to test life cycle-related cases. The injection of mock objects can also facilitate testing of other aspects of the Activity, such as accessing system resources.

Testing files, databases, and content providers

Some test cases have the need to exercise databases or `ContentProvider` operations, and soon comes the need to mock these operations. For example, if we are testing an application on a real device, we don't want to interfere with the normal operation of applications on the said device, especially if we were to change values that may be shared by more than one application.

Such cases can take advantage of another mock class that is not a part of the `android.test.mock` package but of `android.test` instead, namely `RenamingDelegatingContext`.

Remember, this class lets us mock file and database operations. A prefix supplied in the constructor is used to modify the target of these operations. All other operations are delegated to the delegating Context that you specify.

Suppose our Activity under test uses some files or databases that we want to control in some way, probably to introduce specialized content to drive our tests, and we don't want to, or we cannot use the real files or database. In such cases, we create `RenamingDelegatingContext`, which specifies a prefix. We provide mock files using this prefix and introduce any content we need to drive our tests, and the Activity under test could use them with no alteration.

The advantage of keeping our Activity unchanged, that is, not modifying it to read from a different source, is that this assures that all the tests are valid. If we introduce a change only intended for our tests, we will not be able to assure that, under real conditions, the Activity behaves the same.

To demonstrate this case, we will create an extremely simple Activity.

The `MockContextExampleActivity` activity displays the content of a file inside `TextView`. What we intend to demonstrate is how it displays different content during a normal operation of Activity, as compared to when it is under test:

```
public class MockContextExampleActivity extends Activity {
    private static final String FILE_NAME = "my_file.txt";

    private TextView textView;

    @Override
    public void onCreate(Bundle savedInstanceState) {
        super.onCreate(savedInstanceState);
        setContentView(R.layout.activity_mock_context_example);

        textView = (TextView) findViewById(R.id.mock_text_view);
        try {
            FileInputStream fis = openFileInput(FILE_NAME);
            textView.setText(convertStreamToString(fis));
        } catch (FileNotFoundException e) {
            textView.setText("File not found");
        }
    }

    private String convertStreamToString(java.io.InputStream is) {
        Scanner s = new Scanner(is, "UTF-8").useDelimiter("\\A");
        return s.hasNext() ? s.next() : "";
    }

    public String getText() {
        return textView.getText().toString();
    }
}
```

This is our simple Activity. It reads the content of the `my_file.txt` file and displays it on `TextView`. It also displays any error that might occur. Obviously, in a real scenario, you would have better error handling than this.

We need some content for this file. Probably the easiest way to create the files is as shown in the following code:

```
$ adb shell
$ echo "This is real data" > data/data/com.blundell.tut/files/my_file.txt

$ echo "This is *MOCK* data" > /data/data/com.blundell.tut/files/test.
my_file.txt
```

We created two different files, one named my_file.txt and the other test.my_file.txt, with different content. The latter indicates that it is a mock content. If you ran the preceding activity now, you would see **This is real data** as it is reading from the expected file my_file.txt.

The following code demonstrates the use of this mock data in our activity tests:

```java
public class MockContextExampleTest
extends ActivityUnitTestCase<MockContextExampleActivity> {

private static final String PREFIX = "test.";
private RenamingDelegatingContext mockContext;

public MockContextExampleTest() {
super(MockContextExampleActivity.class);
}

@Override
protected void setUp() throws Exception {
super.setUp();
mockContext = new RenamingDelegatingContext(getInstrumentation().
getTargetContext(), PREFIX);
mockContext.makeExistingFilesAndDbsAccessible();
}

public void testSampleTextDisplayed() {
setActivityContext(mockContext);

    startActivity(new Intent(), null, null);

assertEquals("This is *MOCK* data\n", getActivity().getText());
}
}
```

The `MockContextExampleTest` class extends `ActivityUnitTestCase` because we are looking for isolated testing of `MockContextExampleActivity` and because we are going to inject a mocked context; in this case, the injected context is `RenamingDelegatingContext` as a dependency.

Our fixture consists of the mock context, `mockContext` and `RenamingDelegatingContext`, using the target context obtained by `getInstrumentation().getTargetContext()`. Note that the context where the instrumentation is run is different than the context of the Activity under test.

Here a fundamental step follows—since we want to make the existing files and databases accessible to this test, we have to invoke `makeExistingFilesAndDbsAccessible()`.

Then, our test named `testSampleTextDisplayed()` injects the mock context using `setActivityContext()`.

> You must invoke `setActivityContext()` to inject a mock context before you start the Activity under test by invoking `startActivity()`.

Then, the Activity is started by `startActivity()` using a blank Intent just created.

We obtain the text value held by the `TextView` by using a getter that we added to the Activity. I would never recommend changing production code (that is, exposing getters) just for your tests in a real project, as this can lead to bugs, incorrect usage patterns by other developers, and security issues. However, here, we are demonstrating the use of `RenamingDelegatingContext` rather than test correctness.

Finally, the text value obtained is checked against the `This is MOCK*` data string. It is important here to notice that the value used for this test is the test file content and not the real file content.

The BrowserProvider tests

These tests are based on the Browser module of the Android Open Source Project (AOSP). The AOSP has lots of great test examples, and using them as an example here stops you from writing a lot of boilerplate code to set up the scenario for the test. They are intended to test some aspects of the Browser bookmarks, content provider, which is part of the standard Browser included with the Android platform (not the Chrome app but the default Browser app):

```
public class BrowserProviderTests extends AndroidTestCase {
    private List<Uri> deleteUris;

    @Override
```

```
    protected void setUp() throws Exception {
        super.setUp();
        deleteUris = new ArrayList<Uri>();
    }

    @Override
    protected void tearDown() throws Exception {
        for (Uri uri : deleteUris) {
            deleteUri(uri);
        }
        super.tearDown();
    }
}
```

 AOSP tests are not available from the example project with this chapter but are available online at https://github.com/android/ platform_packages_apps_browser/blob/master/tests/src/ com/android/browser/BrowserProviderTests.java.

This snippet includes the test case definition that extends AndroidTestCase. The BrowserProviderTests class extends AndroidTestCase because a Context is needed to access the provider content.

The fixture created in the setUp() method creates a list of Uris that are used to keep track of the inserted Uris to be deleted at the end of each test in the tearDown() method. The developers could have saved this hassle using a mock content provider, maintaining the isolation between our tests and the system. Anyway, tearDown() iterates over this list and deletes the stored Uris. There is no need to override the constructor here as AndroidTestCase is not a parameterized class, and we don't need to do anything special in it.

Now comes the test:

```
public void testHasDefaultBookmarks() {
  Cursor c = getBookmarksSuggest("");
  try {
    assertTrue("No default bookmarks", c.getCount() > 0);
  } finally {
    c.close();
  }
}
```

The `testHasDefaultBookmarks()` method is a test to ensure that there are a number of default bookmarks always present in the database. On startup, a cursor iterates over the default bookmarks obtained by invoking `getBookmarksSuggest("")`, which returns an unfiltered cursor of bookmarks; this is why the content provider query parameter is `""`:

```
public void testPartialFirstTitleWord() {
    assertInsertQuery(
"http://www.example.com/rasdfe", "nfgjra sdfywe", "nfgj");
}
```

The `testPartialFirstTitleWord()` method and three others like it not shown here `testFullFirstTitleWord()`, `testFullFirstTitleWordPartialSecond()`, and `testFullTitle()` test for the insertion of bookmarks. To achieve this, they invoke `assertInsertQuery()` using the bookmarked URL, its title, and the query. The method `assertInsertQuery()` adds the bookmarks to the bookmark provider, inserting the URL issued as a parameter with the specified title. The `Uri` returned is verified to be not null and not exactly the same as the default one. Finally, the `Uri` is inserted in the list of `Uri` instances to be deleted in `tearDown()`. The code for this can be seen in the utility methods shown as follows:

```
public void testFullTitleJapanese() {
    String title = "\u30ae\u30e3\u30e9\u30ea\u30fc\u30fcGoogle\u691c\u7d22";
    assertInsertQuery("http://www.example.com/sdaga", title, title);
}
```

> Unicode is a computing industry standard designed to consistently and uniquely encode characters used in written languages throughout the world. The Unicode standard uses hexadecimals to express a character. For example, the value \u30ae represents the Katakana letter GI (ギ).

We have several tests that are intended to verify the utilization of this bookmark provider for locales and languages other than just English. These particular cases cover the Japanese language utilization in bookmark titles. The tests `testFullTitleJapanese()`, and two others that are not shown here, that is, `testPartialTitleJapanese()` and `testSoundmarkTitleJapanese()` are the Japanese versions of the tests introduced before using Unicode characters. It is recommended to test the application's components under different conditions, like in this case, where other languages with different character sets are used.

Several utility methods follow. These are the utilities used in the tests. We briefly looked at `assertInsertQuery()` before, so now, let's look at the other methods as well:

```
private void assertInsertQuery(String url, String title, String query)
{
        addBookmark(url, title);
        assertQueryReturns(url, title, query);
    }
    private void addBookmark(String url, String title) {
        Uri uri = insertBookmark(url, title);
        assertNotNull(uri);
        assertFalse(BOOKMARKS_URI.equals(uri));
        deleteUris.add(uri);
    }
    private Uri insertBookmark(String url, String title) {
        ContentValues values = new ContentValues();
        values.put("title", title);
        values.put("url", url);
        values.put("visits", 0);
        values.put("date", 0);
        values.put("created", 0);
        values.put("bookmark", 1);
        return getContext().getContentResolver().insert(BOOKMARKS_URI,
values);
    }


    private void assertQueryReturns(String url, String title, String
query) {
  Cursor c = getBookmarksSuggest(query);
  try {
    assertTrue(title + " not matched by " + query, c.getCount() > 0);
    assertTrue("More than one result for " + query, c.getCount() ==
1);
    while (c.moveToNext()) {
      String text1 = getCol(c, SearchManager.SUGGEST_COLUMN_TEXT_1);
      assertNotNull(text1);
      assertEquals("Bad title", title, text1);
      String text2 = getCol(c, SearchManager.SUGGEST_COLUMN_TEXT_2);
      assertNotNull(text2);
      String data = getCol(c, SearchManager.SUGGEST_COLUMN_INTENT_
DATA);
        assertNotNull(data);
```

```
        assertEquals("Bad URL", url, data);
      }
    } finally {
      c.close();
    }
  }

  private String getCol(Cursor c, String name) {
    int col = c.getColumnIndex(name);
    String msg = "Column " + name + " not found, "
                + "columns: " + Arrays.toString(c.getColumnNames()));
    assertTrue(msg, col >= 0);
    return c.getString(col);
  }

  private Cursor getBookmarksSuggest(String query) {
    Uri suggestUri = Uri.parse("content://browser/bookmarks/search_
suggest_query");
    String[] selectionArgs = {query};
    Cursor c = getContext().getContentResolver().query(suggestUri, null,
"url LIKE ?", selectionArgs, null);
    assertNotNull(c);
    return c;
  }

  private void deleteUri(Uri uri) {
    int count = getContext().getContentResolver().delete(uri, null,
null);
    assertEquals("Failed to delete " + uri, 1, count);
  }
```

The method `assertInsertQuery()` invokes `assertQueryReturns(url,
title,` and `query)`, after `addBookmark()`, to verify that the Cursor returned by
`getBookmarksSuggest(query)` contains the expected data. This expectation can
be summarized as:

- The number of rows returned by the query is greater than 0
- The number of rows returned by the query is equal to 1
- The title in the returned row is not null
- The title returned by the query is exactly the same as the method parameter
- The second line for the suggestion is not null
- The URL returned by the query is not null
- This URL matches exactly the URL issued as the method parameter

This strategy provides an interesting pattern to follow in our tests. Some of the utility methods that we need to create to complete our tests can also carry their own verification of several conditions and improve our test quality.

Creating assert methods in our classes allows us to introduce a domain-specific testing language that can be reused when testing other parts of the system.

Testing exceptions

We have mentioned this before in *Chapter 1, Getting Started with Testing*, where we stated that you should test for exceptions and wrong values instead of just testing positive cases:

```
@Test(expected = InvalidTemperatureException.class)
public final void testExceptionForLessThanAbsoluteZeroF() {
  TemperatureConverter.
fahrenheitToCelsius(TemperatureConverter.ABSOLUTE_ZERO_F - 1);
}

@Test(expected = InvalidTemperatureException.class)
public final void testExceptionForLessThanAbsoluteZeroC() {
    TemperatureConverter.
celsiusToFahrenheit(TemperatureConverter.ABSOLUTE_ZERO_C - 1);
}
```

We have also presented these tests before, but here, we are digging deeper into it. The first thing to notice is that these are JUnit4 tests, meaning we can test for exceptions using the `expected` annotation parameter. When you download the chapter's sample project, you will be able to see that it is split into two modules, one of them being core, which is a pure Java module, and so, we have the chance to use JUnit4. At the time of writing this, Android has announced JUnit4 support but not yet released it, so we are still on JUnit3 for Instrumented Android tests.

Every time we have a method that is supposed to generate an exception, we should test this exceptional condition. The best way of doing it is by using JUnit4's `expected` parameter. This declares that the test should throw the exception, if it does not throw the exception or throws a different exception, the test will fail. This can also be done in JUnit3 by invoking the method under test inside a try-catch block, catching the expected exception, and failing otherwise:

```
public void testExceptionForLessThanAbsoluteZeroC() {
    try {
       TemperatureConverter.celsiusToFahrenheit(ABSOLUTE_ZERO_C -
1);
       fail();
    } catch (InvalidTemperatureException ex) {
```

```
                    // do nothing we expect this exception!
                }
        }
}
```

Testing local and remote services

When you want to test an `android.app.Service`, the idea is to extend the `ServiceTestCase<Service>` class to test in a controlled environment:

```
public class DummyServiceTest extends ServiceTestCase<DummyService> {
    public DummyServiceTest() {
        super(DummyService.class);
    }

    public void testBasicStartup() {
        Intent startIntent = new Intent();
        startIntent.setClass(getContext(), DummyService.class);
        startService(startIntent);
    }

    public void testBindable() {
        Intent startIntent = new Intent();
        startIntent.setClass(getContext(), DummyService.class);
        bindService(startIntent);
    }
}
```

The constructor, as in other similar cases, invokes the parent constructor that passes the Android service class as a parameter.

This is followed by `testBasicStartup()`. We start the service using an Intent that we create here, setting its class to the class of the service under test. We also use the instrumented Context for this Intent. This class allows for some dependency injection, as every service depends on the Context in which it runs, and the application with which it is associated. This framework allows you to inject modified, mock, or isolated replacements for these dependencies, and thus performs a true unit test.

> **Dependency Injection (DI)** is a software design pattern that deals with how components get hold of their dependencies. You can do this yourself manually or use one of the many dependency injection libraries.

Since we simply run our tests as is, the service will be injected with a fully functional `Context` and a generic `MockApplication` object. Then, we start the service using the `startService(startIntent)` method, in the same way as if it were started by `Context.startService()`, providing the arguments it supplied. If you use this method to start the service, it will automatically be stopped by `tearDown()`.

Another test, `testBindable()`, will test whether the service can be bound. This test uses `bindService(startIntent)`, which starts the service under test in the same way as if it were started by `Context.bindService()`, providing the arguments it supplied. It returns the communication channel to the service. It may return null if clients cannot bind to the service. Most probably, this test should check for the null return value in the service with an assertion like `assertNotNull(service)` to verify that the service was bound correctly, but it doesn't, so we can focus on the framework classes in use. Be sure to include this test when you write code for similar cases.

The returned `IBinder` is usually for a complex interface that has been described using AIDL. In order to test with this interface, your service must implement a `getService()` method, as shown in `DummService` in the example project for this chapter; which has this implementation of that method:

```
public class LocalBinder extends Binder {
    DummyService getService() {
        return DummyService.this;
    }
}
```

Extensive use of mock objects

In the previous chapters, we described and used the mock classes that are present in the Android SDK. While these classes can cover a great number of cases, there are other Android classes and your own domain classes to consider. You might have the need for other mock objects to furnish your test cases.

Several libraries provide the infrastructure to satisfy our mocking needs, but we are now concentrating on Mockito, which is perhaps the most widely used library in Android.

 This is not a Mockito tutorial. We will just be analyzing its use in Android, so if you are not familiar with it, I would recommend that you take a look at the documentation available on its website at `https://code.google.com/p/mockito/`.

Mockito is an open source software project available under the MIT license, and provides test doubles (mock objects). It is a perfect match for Test-driven Development due to the way it verifies expectations and due to its dynamically generated mock objects because they support refactoring, and the test code will not break when renaming methods or changing its signature.

Summarizing its documentation, the most relevant benefits of Mockito are as follows:

- Ask questions about interactions after execution
- It is not expect-run-verify – avoids expensive setup
- One way to mock that is a simple API
- Easy refactoring with types used
- It mocks concrete classes as well as interfaces

To demonstrate its usage and to establish a style that can be later reproduced for other tests, we are completing some example test cases.

 The latest version of Mockito supported by Android as of this writing is Dexmaker Mockito 1.1. You might want to try out a different one, but you will most probably encounter problems.

The first thing we should do is add `Mockito` as a dependency for your Android instrumentation tests. This is as simple as adding the `androidTestCompile` reference to your dependencies closure. Gradle will do the rest, that is, download the JAR file and add it to your classpath:

```
dependencies {
    // other compile dependencies

    androidTestCompile('com.google.dexmaker:dexmaker-mockito:1.1')
}
```

In order to use Mockito in our tests, we only need to statically import its methods from `org.mockito`. Usually, your IDE will give you the option to statically import these, but if it does not, you can try to add them manually (if the code is red when manually added, then you have a problem with the library being available):

```
import static org.mockito.Matchers.*;
import static org.mockito.Mockito.*;
```

It is preferable to use specific imports instead of using the wildcard. The wildcards are here just for brevity. It is most likely that when your IDE autosaves, it will expand them into the imports needed (or remove them if you aren't using them!).

Importing libraries

We have added the Mockito library to the project's Java Build Path. Usually, this is not a problem, but sometimes, rebuilding the project leads us to the following error that stops the project being built: **Error: duplicate files during packaging of APK**.

This depends on how many libraries are included by the project and what they are.

Most of the available open source libraries have a similar content as proposed by GNU and include files such as LICENSE, NOTICE, CHANGES, COPYRIGHT, and INSTALL, among others. We will find this problem as soon as we try to include more than one in the same project to ultimately build a single APK. This can be resolved in your build.gradle:

```
packagingOptions {
    exclude 'META-INF/LICENSE'
    exclude 'folder/duplicatedFileName'
}
```

Mockito usage example

Let's create EditText, which only accepts signed decimal numbers. We'll call it EditNumber. EditNumber uses InputFilter to provide this feature. In the following tests, we will be exercising this filter to verify that the correct behavior is implemented.

To create the test, we will be using a property that EditNumber inherits from EditText, so it can add a listener, actually a TextWatcher. This will provide methods that are called whenever the text of EditNumber changes. This TextWatcher is a collaborator for the test, and we could have implemented it as its own separate class and verified the results of calling its methods, but this is tedious, and might introduce more errors, so the approach taken is to use Mockito in order to avoid the need of writing an external TextWatcher.

This is precisely how we are introducing a mock TextWatcher to check method invocations when the text changes.

The EditNumber filter tests

This suite of tests will exercise InputFilter behavior of EditNumber, checking the method calls on the TextWatcher mock and verifying the results.

We are using an AndroidTestCase because we are interested in testing EditNumber in isolation of other components or Activities.

We have several inputs that need to be tested (we allow decimal numbers, but do not allow multiple decimals, letters, and so on), and so we can have one test with an array of expected input and an array of expected output. However, the test can get very complicated and would be awful to maintain. A better approach is to have one test for each test case of InputFilter. This allows us to give meaningful names to our tests and an explanation of what we are aiming to test. We will finish up with a list like this:

```
testTextChangedFilter*
        * WorksForBlankInput
        * WorksForSingleDigitInput
        * WorksForMultipleDigitInput
        * WorksForZeroInput
        * WorksForDecimalInput
        * WorksForNegativeInput
        * WorksForDashedInput
        * WorksForPositiveInput
        * WorksForCharacterInput
        * WorksForDoubleDecimalInput
```

Now, we will run through the use of mocks for one of these tests testTextChangedFilterWorksForCharacterInput(), and if you check the example project, you will see that all the other tests follow the same pattern, and we have actually extracted out a helper method that acts as a custom assertion for all tests:

```
public void testTextChangedFilterWorksForCharacterInput() {
    assertEditNumberTextChangeFilter("A1A", "1");
}
/**
 * @param input   the text to be filtered
 * @param output the result you expect once the input has been
filtered
 */
private void assertEditNumberTextChangeFilter(String input, String
output) {
  int lengthAfter = output.length();
  TextWatcher mockTextWatcher = mock(TextWatcher.class);
  editNumber.addTextChangedListener(mockTextWatcher);

  editNumber.setText(input);

  verify(mockTextWatcher)
 .afterTextChanged(editableCharSequenceEq(output));
  verify(mockTextWatcher)
```

```
.onTextChanged(charSequenceEq(output), eq(0), eq(0), eq(lengthAfter));
 verify(mockTextWatcher)
.beforeTextChanged(charSequenceEq(""), eq(0), eq(0), eq(lengthAfter));
}
```

As you can see, the text case is pretty straightforward; it asserts that when you enter A1A into the text of the **EditNumber** view, the text is actually changed into 1. This means that our EditNumber has filtered out the characters. An interesting thing happens when we look at the `assertEditNumberTextChangeFilter(inp ut, output)` helper method. Within our helper method is where we verify that the `InputFilter` is doing its job and it is here we use Mockito. There are four common steps to take when using Mockito mock objects:

1. Instantiate the intended mocks that are ready for use.
2. Determine what behavior is expected and stub it to return any fixture data.
3. Exercise the methods, usually by invoking methods of the class under test.
4. Verify the behavior of your mock object to pass the test.

According to step one, we create a mock `TextWatcher` using `mock(TextWatcher. class)` and set it as our `TextChangedListener` on EditNumber.

We skip step two in this instance as we have no fixture data, in that the class we are mocking does not have any methods that are expected to return a value. We'll come back to this in another test later on.

In step three, we have our mock in place, and we can exercise the method under test to perform its intended action. In our case, the method is `editNumber. setText(input)`, and the intended action is to set the text and thus prompt our `InputFilter` to run.

Step four is where we verify that the text was actually changed by our filter. Let's break step four down a little. Here are our verifications again:

```
verify(mockTextWatcher)
.afterTextChanged(editableCharSequenceEq(output));
verify(mockTextWatcher)
.onTextChanged(charSequenceEq(output), eq(0), eq(0), eq(lengthAfter));
verify(mockTextWatcher)
.beforeTextChanged(charSequenceEq(""), eq(0), eq(0), eq(lengthAfter));
```

We will be using two custom written matchers (`editableCharSequenceEq(String)` and `charSequenceEq(String)`) because we are interested in comparing the string content for different classes used by Android, such as `Editable` and `CharSequence`. When you use a special matcher, it means all comparisons done for that verification method call need a special wrapper method.

The other matcher, `eq()`, expects `int` that is equal to the given value. The latter is provided by Mockito for all primitive types and objects, but we need to implement `editableCharSequenceEq()` and `charSequenceEq()` as it is an Android-specific matcher.

Mockito has a predefined `ArgumentMatcher` that would help us create our matcher. You extend the class and it gives you one method to override:

```
abstract boolean matches(T t);
```

The `matches` argument matcher method expects an argument that you can use to compare against a predefined variable. This argument is the "actual" result of your method invocation, and the predefined variable is the "expected" one. You then decide to return true or false whether they are the same or not.

As you might have already realized, the custom `ArgumentMatcher` class's frequent use in a test could become really complex and might lead to errors, so to simplify this process, we will be using a helper class that we call `CharSequenceMatcher`. We also have `EditableCharSequenceMatcher`, which can be found in the example project of this chapter:

```java
class CharSequenceMatcher extends ArgumentMatcher<CharSequence> {

    private final CharSequence expected;

    static CharSequence charSequenceEq(CharSequence expected) {
        return argThat(new CharSequenceMatcher(expected));
    }

    CharSequenceMatcher(CharSequence expected) {
        this.expected = expected;
    }

    @Override
    public boolean matches(Object actual) {
        return expected.toString().equals(actual.toString());
    }

    @Override
    public void describeTo(Description description) {
        description.appendText(expected.toString());
    }
}
```

We implement matches by returning the result of the comparison of the object passed as arguments with our predefined field after they are converted to a string.

We also override the `describeTo` method, and this allows us to change the error message when the verification fails. This is always a good tip to remember: take a look at the error messages before and after doing this:

```
Argument(s) are different! Wanted:
textWatcher.afterTextChanged(<Editable char sequence matcher>);
Actual invocation has different arguments:
textWatcher.afterTextChanged(1);


Argument(s) are different! Wanted:
textWatcher.afterTextChanged(1XX);
Actual invocation has different arguments:
textWatcher.afterTextChanged(1);
```

When the static instantiation method for our matcher is used and we import this as a static method, in our test, we can simply write:

```
verify(mockTextWatcher).onTextChanged(charSequenceEq(output), …
```

Testing views in isolation

The test that we are analyzing here is based on the Focus2AndroidTest from the Android SDK ApiDemos project. It demonstrates how some properties of the Views that conform to a layout can be tested when the behavior itself cannot be isolated. The testing focusability of a view is one of these situations.

We are only testing individual views. In order to avoid creating the full Activity, this test extends `AndroidTestCase`. You may have thought about using just `TestCase`, but unfortunately, this is not possible as we need a Context to inflate the XML layout via `LayoutInflater`, and `AndroidTestCase` will provide us with this component:

```
public class FocusTest extends AndroidTestCase {
  private FocusFinder focusFinder;

  private ViewGroup layout;

  private Button leftButton;
  private Button centerButton;
  private Button rightButton;

@Override
protected void setUp() throws Exception {
  super.setUp();

  focusFinder = FocusFinder.getInstance();
```

```
// inflate the layout
Context context = getContext();
LayoutInflater inflater = LayoutInflater.from(context);
layout = (ViewGroup) inflater.inflate(R.layout.view_focus, null);

// manually measure it, and lay it out
layout.measure(500, 500);
layout.layout(0, 0, 500, 500);

leftButton = (Button) layout.findViewById(R.id.focus_left_button);
centerButton = (Button) layout.findViewById(R.id.focus_center_
button);
rightButton = (Button) layout.findViewById(R.id.focus_right_button);
}
```

The setup prepares our test as follows:

1. We request a `FocusFinder` class. This is a class that provides the algorithm used to find the next focusable View. It implements the singleton pattern and that's why we use `FocusFinder.getInstance()` to obtain a reference to it. This class has several methods to help us find focusable and touchable items, given various conditions as the nearest in a given direction or searching from a particular rectangle.

2. Then, we get the `LayoutInflater` class and inflate the layout under test. One thing we need to take into account, as our test is isolated from other parts of the system, is that we have to manually measure and lay out the components.

3. Then, we use the find views pattern and assign the found views to the fields.

In a previous chapter, we enumerated all the available asserts in our arsenal, and you may remember that to test a View's position, we had a complete set of assertions in the `ViewAsserts` class. However, this depends on how the layout is defined:

```
public void testGoingRightFromLeftButtonJumpsOverCenterToRight() {
  View actualNextButton =
focusFinder.findNextFocus(layout, leftButton, View.FOCUS_RIGHT);
  String msg = "right should be next focus from left";
  assertEquals(msg, this.rightButton, actualNextButton);
}

public void testGoingLeftFromRightButtonGoesToCenter() {
  View actualNextButton =
focusFinder.findNextFocus(layout, rightButton, View.FOCUS_LEFT);
  String msg = "center should be next focus from right";
```

```
    assertEquals(msg, this.centerButton, actualNextButton);
}
```

The method `testGoingRightFromLeftButtonJumpsOverCenterToRight()`, as its name suggests, tests the focus gained by the right button when the focus moves from the left to the right button. To achieve this search, the instance of `FocusFinder` obtained during the `setUp()` method is employed. This class has a `findNextFocus()` method to obtain the View that receives focus in a given direction. The value obtained is checked against our expectations.

In a similar way, the `testGoingLeftFromRightButtonGoesToCenter()` test tests the focus that goes in the other direction.

Testing parsers

There are many occasions where your Android application relies on external XML, JSON messages, or documents obtained from web services. These documents are used for data interchange between the local application and the server. There are many use cases where XML or JSON documents are obtained from the server or generated by the local application to be sent to the server. Ideally, methods invoked by these activities have to be tested in isolation to have real unit tests, and to achieve this, we need to include some mock files somewhere in our APK to run the tests.

But the question is where can we include these files?

Let's find out.

Android assets

To begin, a brief review of the assets' definition can be found in the Android SDK documentation:

> *The difference between "resources" and "assets" isn't much on the surface, but in general, you'll use resources to store your external content much more often than you'll use assets. The real difference is that anything placed in the resources directory will be easily accessible from your application from the R class, which is compiled by Android. Whereas, anything placed in the assets directory will maintain its raw file format and, in order to read it, you must use the AssetManager to read the file as a stream of bytes. So keeping files and data in resources (res/) makes them easily accessible.*

Clearly, assets are what we need to store the files that will be parsed to test the parser.

So our XML or JSON files should be placed in the assets folder to prevent manipulation at compile time and to be able to access the raw content while the application or tests are run.

But be careful, we need to place them in the assets of our `androidTest` folder because then, these are not part of the application, and we don't want them packed with our code when we release a live application.

The parser test

This test implements an `AndroidTestCase` as all we need is a Context to be able to reference our assets folder. Also, we have written the parsing inside of the test, as the point of this test is not how to parse xml but how to reference mock assets from your tests:

```
public class ParserExampleActivityTest extends AndroidTestCase {

 public void testParseXml() throws IOException {
 InputStream assetsXml = getContext().getAssets()
.open("my_document.xml");

  String result = parseXml(assetsXml);
  assertNotNull(result);
 }
}
}
```

The `InputStream` class is obtained by opening the `my_document.xml` file from the assets by `getContext().getAssets()`. Note that the Context and thus the assets obtained here are from the tests package and not from the Activity under test.

Next, the `parseXml()` method is invoked using the recently obtained `InputStream`. If there is an `IOException`, the test will fail and spit out the error from the stack trace, and if everything goes well, we test that the result is not null.

We should then provide the XML we want to use for the test in an asset named `my_document.xml`. You want the asset to be under the test project folder; by default, this is `androidTest/assets`.

The content could be:

```
<?xml version="1.0" encoding="UTF-8" ?>
<records>
  <record>
    <name>Paul</name>
  </record>
</records>
```

Testing for memory usage

Sometimes, memory consumption is an important factor to measure the good behavior of the test target, be it an Activity, Service, Content Provider, or another component.

To test for this condition, we can use a utility test that you can invoke from other tests mainly after having run a test loop:

```
public void assertNotInLowMemoryCondition() {
//Verification: check if it is in low memory
ActivityManager.MemoryInfo mi = new ActivityManager.MemoryInfo();
  ((ActivityManager)getActivity()
.getSystemService(Context.ACTIVITY_SERVICE)).getMemoryInfo(mi);
assertFalse("Low memory condition", mi.lowMemory);
}
```

This assertion can be called from other tests. At the beginning, it obtains `MemoryInfo` from `ActivityManager` using `getMemoryInfo()`, after getting the instance using `getSystemService()`. The `lowMemory` field is set to `true` if the system considers itself to currently be in a low memory situation.

In some cases, we want to dive even deeper into the resource usage and can obtain more detailed information from the process table.

We can create another helper method to obtain process information and use it in our tests:

```
        private String captureProcessInfo() {
            InputStream in = null;
            try {
                String cmd = "ps";
                Process p = Runtime.getRuntime().exec(cmd);
                in = p.getInputStream();
                Scanner scanner = new Scanner(in);
                scanner.useDelimiter("\\A");
                return scanner.hasNext() ? scanner.next() : "scanner
error";
            } catch (IOException e) {
                fail(e.getLocalizedMessage());
            } finally {
                if (in != null) {
                    try {
                        in.close();
                    } catch (IOException ignore) {
                    }
                }
```

```
        }
        return "captureProcessInfo error";
}
```

To obtain this information, a command (in this case, `ps` is used, but you can adapt it to your needs) is executed using `Runtime.exec()`. The output of this command is concatenated in a string that is later returned. We can use the return value to print it to the logs in our test, or we can further process the content to obtain summary information.

This is an example of logging the output:

```
Log.d(TAG, captureProcessInfo());
```

When this test is run, we obtain information about the running processes:

D/ActivityTest(1): USER	PID	PPID	VSIZE	RSS	WCHAN	PC	NAME
D/ActivityTest(1): root /init	1	0	312	220	c009b74c	0000ca4c	S
D/ActivityTest(1): root kthreadd	2	0	0	0	c004e72c	00000000	S
D/ActivityTest(1): root ksoftirqd/0	3	2	0	0	c003fdc8	00000000	S
D/ActivityTest(1): root events/0	4	2	0	0	c004b2c4	00000000	S
D/ActivityTest(1): root khelper	5	2	0	0	c004b2c4	00000000	S
D/ActivityTest(1): root suspend	6	2	0	0	c004b2c4	00000000	S
D/ActivityTest(1): root kblockd/0	7	2	0	0	c004b2c4	00000000	S
D/ActivityTest(1): root cqueue	8	2	0	0	c004b2c4	00000000	S
D/ActivityTest(1): root kseriod	9	2	0	0	c018179c	00000000	S

The output was cut for brevity, but if you run it, you will get the complete list of processes that run on the system.

A brief explanation of the information obtained is as follows:

Column	Description
USER	This is the textual user ID.
PID	This is the process ID number of the process.
PPID	This is the parent process ID.
VSIZE	This is the virtual memory size of the process in KB. This is the virtual memory the process reserves.
RSS	This is the resident set size, the non-swapped physical memory that a task has used (in pages). This is the actual amount of real memory the process takes in pages. This does not include pages that have not been demand-loaded in.
WCHAN	This is the "channel" in which the process is waiting. It is the address of a system call, and can be looked up in a name list if you need a textual name.
PC	This is the current EIP (instruction pointer).
State (no header)	This denotes the process states, which are as follows: • S is used to indicate sleeping in an interruptible state • R is used to indicate running • T is used to indicate a stopped process • Z is used to indicate a zombie
Column	Description
NAME	This denotes the command name. The application processes in Android are renamed after its package name.

Testing with Espresso

Testing UI components can be difficult. Knowing when a view has been inflated or ensuring you don't access views on the wrong thread can lead to strange behavior and flaky tests. This is why Google has released a helper library for UI-related instrumentation tests called Espresso (`https://code.google.com/p/android-test-kit/wiki/Espresso`).

Adding the Espresso library JAR can be achieved by adding to the `/libs` folder, but to make it easier for Gradle users, Google released a version to their Maven repository (consider yourselves lucky users because this was not available before version 2.0). When using Espresso, you need to use the bundled TestRunner as well. Therefore, the setup becomes:

```
dependencies {
// other dependencies
```

```
androidTestCompile('com.android.support.test.espresso:espresso-
core:2.0')
}
android {
    defaultConfig {
    // other configuration
    testInstrumentationRunner "android.support.test.runner.
AndroidJUnitRunner"
    }
    // Annoyingly there is a overlap with Espresso dependencies at the
    moment
    // add this closure to fix internal jar file name clashes
    packagingOptions {
        exclude 'LICENSE.txt'
    }
}
```

Once the Espresso dependency has been added to your project, you have a fluid interface to be able to assert the behavior on your UI elements. In our example, we have an Activity that allows you to order Espresso coffee. When you press the order button, a nice Espresso image appears. We want to verify this behavior in an instrumentation test.

The first thing to do is to set up our Activity to test. We use `ActivityInstrumentationTestCase2` so that we can have a full lifecycle Activity running. You need to call `getActivity()` at the start of your test or in the `setup()` method to allow the activity to be started and for Espresso to find the Activity in a resumed state:

```
public class ExampleEspressoTest extends ActivityInstrumentationTestCa
se2<EspressoActivity> {

    public ExampleEspressoTest() {
        super(EspressoActivity.class);
    }

    @Override
    public void setUp() throws Exception {
        getActivity();
    }
```

Once the setup is done, we can write a test using Espresso to click our button and check whether the image was shown (made visible) in the Activity:

```
public void testClickingButtonShowsImage() {
    Espresso.onView(
            ViewMatchers.withId(R.id.espresso_button_order))
            perform(ViewActions.click());

    Espresso.onView(
            ViewMatchers.withId(R.id.espresso_imageview_cup))
                .check(ViewAssertions.matches(ViewMatchers.
    isDisplayed()));
    }
```

This example shows the use of Espresso to find our order button, click on the button, and check whether our ordered Espresso is shown to the user. Espresso has a fluid interface, meaning it follows a builder-style pattern, and most method calls can be chained. In the preceding example, I showed the fully qualified classes for clarity, but these can easily be changed to static imports so that the test is even more human readable:

```
public void testClickingButtonShowsImage() {
    onView(withId(R.id.espresso_button_order))
            .perform(click());

    onView(withId(R.id.espresso_imageview_cup))
            .check(matches(isDisplayed()));
}
```

This can now be read in a much more *sentence* style. This example shows the use of Espresso to find our order button `onView(withId(R.id.espresso_button_order))`. Click on `perform(click())`, then we find the cup image `onView(withId(R.id.espresso_imageview_cup))`, and check whether it is visible to the user `check(matches(isDisplayed()))`.

This shows that the only classes you need to think about are:

- **Espresso**: This is the entry point. Always start with this to interact with a View.
- **ViewMatchers**: This is used to locate a View within the current hierarchy.
- **ViewActions**: This is used to click, long click, and so on, on a located View.
- **ViewAssertions**: This is used to check the state of a View after an action has been performed.

Espresso has a really powerful API, which allows you to test the positions of views next to each other, match data in a ListView, get data straight from a header or footer, and check the views in your ActionBar/ToolBar and many more assertions. Another feature is its capability to deal with threading; Espresso will wait for asynchronous tasks to finish before it asserts whether the UI has changed. An explanation of these features and much more is listed on the wiki page (`https://code.google.com/p/android-test-kit/w/list`).

Summary

In this chapter, several real-world examples of tests that cover a wide range of cases were presented. You can use them as a starting point while creating your own tests.

We covered a variety of testing recipes that you can extend for your own tests. We used mock contexts and showed how `RenamingDelegatingContext` can be used in various situations to change the data obtained by the tests. We also analyzed the injection of these mock contexts into test dependencies.

Then, we used `ActivityUnitTestCase` to test Activities in complete isolation. We tested Views in isolation using `AndroidTestCase`. We demonstrated the use of Mockito to mock objects combined with `ArgumentMatchers` to provide custom matchers on any object. Finally, we treated the analysis of potential memory leaks and took a peek into the power of testing UI with Espresso.

The next chapter focuses on managing your test environment to enable you to run tests in a consistent, fast, and always deterministic way, which leads to automation and those mischievous monkeys!

4
Managing Your Android Testing Environment

Now that we have a complete understanding of the available Android testing SDK and have a nice range of testing recipes ready to assert and verify our app's behavior, it is time to provide different conditions to run our tests, explore other tests, or even use the application manually to understand what the end user experience would be.

In this chapter, we will cover:

- Creating Android Virtual Devices (AVD) to provide different conditions and configurations for an application
- Understanding the different configurations that we can specify while creating AVDs
- How to run AVDs
- How to create headless emulators
- Unlocking the screen to be able to run all the tests
- Simulating real-life network conditions
- Speeding up your AVD with HAXM
- Alternatives to the Android Virtual Device
- Running monkey to generate events to send to the application

Creating Android Virtual Devices

To have the best chance of detecting problems related to the device on which the application is running, you need the widest possible coverage of device features and configurations.

While final and conclusive tests should always be run on real devices, with the ever-increasing number of devices and form factors, it is virtually impossible that you will have one device of each to test your application. There are also device farms in the cloud to test on a variety of devices (Google for `cloud device testing`), but sometimes, their cost is above the average developer budget. Android provides a way of emulating, more or less verbatim, a great variety of features and configuration just for the convenience of different AVD configurations (an emulator).

 All the examples in this chapter are run from OSX 10.9.4 (Mavericks) 32 bit using Android SDK Tools 23.0.5 with platform 4.4.2 (API 20) installed.

To create an AVD, you can use the `android avd` command from a terminal, or from inside Android Studio, using **Tools | Android | AVD Manager** or its shortcut icon. If you run the AVD Manager from a terminal, you get a GUI that is slightly different than what you get by running from Android Studio, but they both do the same job. We're going to be using the AVD Manager from Android Studio as this is the most likely use case.

By clicking on the icon, you can access the **AVD Manager**. Here, you press the **Create Device...** button to create a new AVD, and the following dialog box is presented:

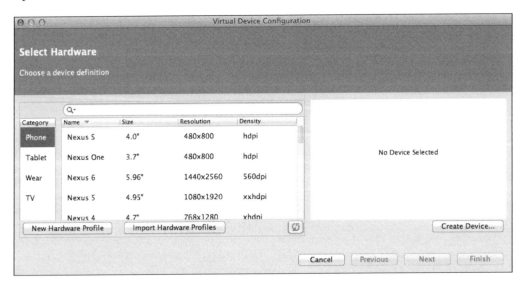

Now, you can select a profile phone for the hardware (let's pick Nexus 5), hit **Next**, and select an Android version (KitKat x86). Hit **Next** again, and you get a summary of your device. You can click on **Finish** and you create the AVD using the default values. However, if you need to support specific configurations, you can specify different hardware properties. Let's change the AVD name to `testdevice`. Even more properties are available by using the **Show Advanced Settings** button.

A wide range of properties can be set. Some highlights are:

- Ram size / SD card size
- Emulate or use your webcam as front / back camera
- Change the network speed / simulate latency

Setting the scale is also very useful to test your application in a window that resembles the size of a real device. It is a very common mistake to test your application in an AVD with a window size that is at least twice the size of a real device, and using a mouse pointer, believing that everything is fine, to later realize on a physical device with a screen of 5 or 6 inches that some items on the UI are impossible to touch with your finger.

Finally, it is also helpful to test your application under the same conditions repeatedly. To be able to test under the same conditions again and again, it is sometimes helpful to delete all the information that was entered in the previous sessions. If this is the case, ensure **Store a snapshot for faster startup** is unticked so as to start afresh every time.

Running AVDs from the command line

Wouldn't it be nice if we could run different AVDs from the command line and perhaps automate the way we run or script our tests?

By freeing the AVD from its UI window, we open a whole new world of automation and scripting possibilities.

Well, let's explore these alternatives.

Headless emulator

A headless emulator (its UI window is not displayed) comes in very handy when we run automated tests and nobody is looking at the window, or the interaction between the test runner and the application is so fast that we hardly see anything.

Also, it is worth mentioning that, sometimes, you can't understand why some tests fail until you see the interaction on the screen, so use your own judgment when selecting a running mode for your emulator.

One thing that we may have noticed while running AVDs is that their network communication ports are assigned at runtime, incrementing the last used port by 2 and starting with 5554. This is used to name the emulator and set its serial number; for example, the emulator using port 5554 becomes emulator-5554. This is very useful when we run AVDs during the development process because we don't have to pay attention to port assignment. However, it can be very confusing and difficult to track which test runs on which emulator if we are running more than one simultaneously.

In such cases, we will be specifying manual ports to keep the specific AVD under our control.

Usually, when we are running tests on more than one emulator at the same time, not only do we want to detach the window, but also avoid sound output. We will add options for this as well.

The command line to launch the test AVD that we just created is as follows, and the port must be an integer between 5554 and 5584:

```
$ emulator -avd testdevice -no-window -no-audio -no-boot-anim -port 5580
```

We can now check whether the device is in the device list:

```
$ adb devices
List of devices attached
emulator-5580  device
```

The next step is to install the application and the tests:

```
$ adb -s emulator-5580 install YourApp.apk
347 KB/s (16632 bytes in 0.046s) : /data/local/tmp/YourApp.apk
Success
$ adb -s emulator-5580 install YourAppTests.apk
222 KB/s (16632 bytes in 0.072s)
  pkg: /data/local/tmp/YourAppTests.apk
Success
```

Then, we can use the specified serial number to run the tests on it:

```
$ adb -s emulator-5580 shell am instrument -w\
com.blundell.tut.test/android.test.InstrumentationTestRunner
com.blundell.tut.test.MyTests:......
com.blundell.tut.test.MyOtherTests:..........
Test results for InstrumentationTestRunner=.................
Time: 15.295
OK (20 tests)
```

Disabling the keyguard

We can see the tests being run without them requiring any intervention and access to the emulator GUI.

Sometimes, you might receive some errors for tests that are not failing if you run in a more standard approach, like in a standard emulator launched from your IDE. In such cases, one of the reasons is that the emulator might be locked at the first screen, and we need to unlock it to be able to run tests that involve the UI.

To unlock the screen, you can use the following command:

```
$ adb -s emulator-5580 emu event send EV_KEY:KEY_MENU:1 EV_KEY:KEY_MENU:0
```

The lock screen can also be disabled programmatically. In the instrumentation test class, you should add the following code, most probably in `setup()`:

```
@Override
public void setUp() throws Exception {
  Activity activity = getActivity();
  Window window = activity.getWindow();
  window.addFlags(WindowManager.LayoutParams.FLAG_DISMISS_KEYGUARD);
}
```

This will dismiss the keyguard for these tests and has the added advantage of not needing any extra security permissions or changes to the app under test (which the deprecated alternative does, see `http://developer.android.com/reference/android/app/KeyguardManager.html`).

Cleaning up

On certain occasions, you also need to clean up services and processes that are started after running tests. This prevents the results of the latter from being influenced by the ending conditions of the previous tests. In these cases, it is always better to start from a known condition, freeing all the used memory, stopping services, reloading resources, and restarting processes, which is achievable by warm-booting the emulator:

```
$ adb -s emulator-5580 shell 'stop'; sleep 5; start'
```

This command line opens the emulator shell for our emulator, and runs the stop and start commands, or as people say, turning it off and on again.

The output of these commands can be monitored using the `logcat` command:

```
$ adb -s emulator-5580 logcat
```

You will see messages like these:

```
D/AndroidRuntime(1):
D/AndroidRuntime(1): >>>>>>>>>> AndroidRuntime START <<<<<<<<<<
D/AndroidRuntime(1): CheckJNI is ON
D/AndroidRuntime(1): --- registering native functions ---
I/SamplingProfilerIntegration(1): Profiler is disabled.
I/Zygote   (1): Preloading classes...
I/ServiceManager(2): service 'connectivity''connectivity''connectivity'''
died
I/ServiceManager(2): service 'throttle''throttle''throttle''' died
I/ServiceManager(2): service 'accessibility''accessibility''accessibili
ty''' died
```

Terminating the emulator

Once we finish working with one of the headless emulator instances, we start using the command mentioned earlier. We use the following command line to kill it:

```
$ adb -s emulator-5580 emu kill
```

This will stop the emulator from freeing the used resources and terminating the emulator process on the host computer.

Additional emulator configurations

Sometimes, what we need to test is outside the reach of the options that can be set when the AVD is created or configured.

One of the cases could be the need to test our application under different locales. Let's say we want to test our application on a Japanese phone—an emulator, with the language and country set to Japanese and Japan respectively.

We have the ability to pass these properties in the emulator command line. The -prop command line option allows us to set any of the properties we could set:

```
$ emulator -avd testdevice -no-window -no-audio -no-boot-anim -port 5580
-prop persist.sys.language=ja -prop persist.sys.country=JP
```

To verify that our settings were successful, we can use the getprop command to verify them, for example:

```
$ adb -s emulator-5580 shell "getprop persist.sys.language"
ja
$ adb -s emulator-5580 shell "getprop persist.sys.country"
JP
```

If you want to clear all the user data after playing with the persistent settings, you can use the following command:

```
$ adb -s emulator-5580 emu kill
$ emulator -avd testdevice -no-window -no-audio -no-boot-anim -port 5580
-wipe-data
```

After this, the emulator will start afresh.

 More information and a list of available properties for setting the emulator hardware options can be found at http://developer. android.com/tools/devices/managing-avds-cmdline. html#hardwareopts.

Simulating network conditions

It is extremely important to test under different network conditions, but it is neglected more often than not. This can lead to misconceptions that the application behaves differently because we use the host network that presents a different speed and latency.

The Android emulator supports network throttling, for example, to support slower network speeds and higher connection latencies. This can be selected when you first create your AVD, but can also be done in the emulator at any time from the command line using the -netspeed <speed> and -netdelay <delay> options.

The complete list of supporting options is as follows:

For network speed:

Option	Description	Speeds [kbits/s]
-netspeed gsm	GSM/CSD	Up: 14.4, down: 14.4
-netspeed hscsd	HSCSD	Up: 14.4, down: 43.2
-netspeed gprs	GPRS	Up: 40.0, down: 80.0
-netspeed edge	EDGE/EGPRS	Up: 118.4, down: 236.8
-netspeed umts	UMTS/3G	Up: 128.0, down: 1920.0
-netspeed hsdpa	HSDPA	Up: 348.0, down: 14400.0
-netspeed full	No limit	Up: 0.0, down: 0.0
-netspeed <num>	Select both the upload and download speed	Up: as specified, down: as specified
-netspeed <up>:<down>	Select the individual up and down speed	Up: as specified, down: as specified

For latency:

Option	Description	Delay [msec]
`-netdelay gprs`	GPRS	Min 150, max 550
`-netdelay edge`	EDGE/EGPRS	Min 80, max 400
`-netdelay umts`	UMTS/3G	Min 35, max 200
`-netdelay none`	No latency	Min 0, max 0
`-netdelay <num>`	Select exact latency	Latency as specified
`-netdelay <min>:<max>`	Select min and max latencies	Minimum and maximum latencies as specified

If the values are not specified, the emulator uses the following default values:

- The default network speed is full
- The default network latency is none

This is an example of an emulator using these options to select the GSM network speed of 14.4 kbits/sec and a GPRS latency of 150 to 500 msecs:

```
$ emulator -avd testdevice -port 5580 -netspeed gsm -netdelay gprs
```

Once the emulator is running, you can verify these network settings or change them interactively using the Android console inside a Telnet client:

```
$ telnet localhost 5580
Trying 127.0.0.1...
Connected to localhost.
Escape character is '^]'.
Android Console: type 'help' for a list of commands
OK
```

After we are connected, we can type the following command:

```
network status
Current network status:
  download speed:      14400 bits/s (1.8 KB/s)
  upload speed:        14400 bits/s (1.8 KB/s)
  minimum latency:   150 ms
  maximum latency:   550 ms
OK
```

You can use the emulator to test applications using network services either manually or in an automated way.

In some cases, this not only involves throttling the network speed but also changing the state of the GPRS connection to investigate how the application behaves and copes with these situations. To change this status, we can also use the Android console in a running emulator.

For example, to unregister the emulator from the network, we can use:

```
$ telnet localhost 5580
```

After receiving the **OK** subprompt, we can set the data network mode as unregistered by issuing the following command. This will turn off all data:

```
gsm data unregistered
OK
quit
Connection closed by foreign host.
```

After testing the application under this condition, you can connect it again by using the following command line:

```
gsm data home
OK
```

To verify the status, you can use the following command lines:

```
gsm status
gsm voice state: home

gsm data state:   home

OK
```

Speeding up your AVD with HAXM

When using Android Virtual Devices, you'll notice that they aren't the most responsive of emulators. This is due to the fact that the AVD emulator does not support hardware GL, and so the GL code gets translated into ARM software, which gets run on hardware emulated by QEMU (QEMU is the hosted virtual machine monitor that AVDs run on top of). Google has been working on this problem, and now, efficient use of the host GPU is boosting speed (SDK 17). Responsiveness has improved on this and above levels of emulator.

Another speed boost can be gained by using Intel's Hardware Accelerated Execution Manager (HAXM). You can get a 5 to 10 times speed boost on your AVDs that run x86 as it will execute the CPU commands natively.

HAXM works by allowing the CPU commands to be run on your hardware (that is your Intel CPU), whereas earlier, QEMU would be simulating the CPU, and all commands would be through software, which is why the original architecture is cumbersome.

As per the requirements, you need to have an Intel-based processor with VT (Virtualization Technology) support and an x86-based emulator with minimum SDK 10 (Gingerbread). Intel claims that most Intel processors from 2005 onwards will support VT offloading as standard.

Installation is straightforward; download HAXM from the extras section of the Android SDK Manager, locate the downloaded file, and follow the installer instructions. You can clarify a successful installation by running this command from a terminal:

```
kextstat | grep intel
```

If you get a message that contains `com.intel.kext.intelhaxm`, you've installed and can now run your speedy x86 emulator. There is nothing else you have to do, just ensure the CPU/ABI of your Android emulator is x86 and HAXM will be running in the background for you.

Alternatives to the AVD

The Android Virtual Device is not your only way of running Android apps. There are now a few solutions you can choose from. A quick search on Google can bring up this list (I won't write it here as they can quickly get out of date). One of these that I personally recommend is the GenyMotion emulator. This is an Android emulator that uses x86 architecture virtualization to make it much more efficient. It runs much faster and smoother than the AVD. The downside being it is only free for personal use, and as of this writing, it does not emulate all the sensors of a device, but I know they are busy working on this.

Running monkey

You might know about the infinite monkey theorem. This theorem states that a monkey that hits keys at random on a typewriter keyboard for an infinite amount of time will eventually type a given text, such as the complete works of William Shakespeare. The Android version of this theorem states that a monkey that produces random touches on a device could crash your application in, well, much less than an infinite amount of time.

With this, Android features a monkey application (`http://goo.gl/LSWg85`) that will generate the random events instead of a real monkey.

The simplest way to run monkey against our application to generate random events is:

```
$ adb -e shell monkey -p com.blundell.tut -v -v 1000
```

You will be receiving this output:

```
Events injected: 1000
:Sending rotation degree=0, persist=false
:Dropped: keys=0 pointers=4 trackballs=0 flips=0 rotations=0
## Network stats: elapsed time=2577ms (0ms mobile, 0ms wifi, 2577ms not
connected)
// Monkey finished
```

The monkey will send events only to the specified package (`-p`), in this case `com.blundell.tut`, in a very verbose manner (`-v -v`). The count of events sent will be 1000.

The client-server monkey

There is another way of running monkey. It also presents a client-server model that ultimately allows for the creation of scripts that control what events are sent and does not rely only on random generation.

Usually, the port used by monkey is `1080`, but you can use another one if it better suits your preferences:

```
$ adb -e shell monkey -p com.blundell.tut --port 1080 &
```

Then, we need to redirect the emulator port:

```
$ adb -e forward tcp:1080 tcp:1080
```

Now, we are ready to send events. To do it manually, we can use a Telnet client:

```
$ telnet localhost 1080
```

After the connection is established, we can type the specific monkey command:

```
tap 150 200
OK
```

To finish, exit the telnet command.

If we need to exercise the application repeatedly, it is much more convenient to create a script with the commands we want to send. A monkey script could look like this:

```
# monkey
tap 200 200
type HelloWorld
tap 200 350
tap 200 200
press DEL
press DEL
press DEL
press DEL
press DEL
type Monkey
tap 200 350
```

> The API for monkey tap is `tap <x pixel position> <y pixel position>`.
>
> Therefore, if you are not running an emulator with the same § resolution as the one your monkey command was recorded with, you could get incorrect touch events from your monkey.

After having started the example application for this chapter, we can run this script to exercise the user interface. To start the application, you can use the emulator window and click on its launcher icon or use the command line that states the activity you want to start, which is the only alternative if the emulator is headless, as follows:

```
$ adb shell am start -n com.blundell.tut/.MonkeyActivity
```

This is informed in the log by this line:

```
Starting: Intent { cmp=com.blundell.tut/.MonkeyActivity}
```

Once the application has started, you can send the events using the script and the `netcat` utility:

```
$ nc localhost 1080 < ch_4_code_ex_10.txt
```

This will send the events contained in the script file to the emulator. These are the following events:

1. Touch and select the edit text input.
2. Type `Hello World`.
3. Tap the button to show the toast.
4. Touch and select the edit text again.
5. Delete its content.
6. Type `Monkey`.
7. Tap the button to show the toast **Hello Monkey**.

In this manner, simple scripts that consist of touch events and key presses can be created.

Test scripting with monkeyrunner

The possibilities of monkey are fairly limited, and the lack of flow control restricts its use to very simple cases. To circumvent these limitations, a new project was created, which was named monkeyrunner. Notwithstanding this, the name is almost the same and leads to a huge amount of confusion because they are not related in any way.

Monkeyrunner, which is already included in the latest versions of the Android SDK, is a tool that provides an API for the purpose of writing scripts that externally control an Android device or emulator.

Monkeyrunner is built on top of Jython (`http://jython.org/`), a version of the Python programming language (`http://python.org/`), which is designed to run on the Java platform.

According to its documentation, the monkeyrunner tool provides these unique features for Android testing. These are just the highlights of the complete list of features, examples, and reference documentation that can be obtained from the monkeyrunner home page (`http://developer.android.com/tools/help/monkeyrunner_concepts.html`):

*   **Multiple device control**: The `monkeyrunner` API can apply one or more test suites across multiple devices or emulators. You can physically attach all the devices or start up all the emulators (or both) at once, connect to each one in turn programmatically, and then run one or more tests. You can also start up an emulator configuration programmatically, run one or more tests, and then shut down the emulator.

- **Functional testing**: monkeyrunner can run an automated start-to-finish test of an Android application. You provide input values with keystrokes or touch events, and view the results as screenshots.

- **Regression testing**: monkeyrunner can test the application stability by running an application and comparing its output screenshots to a set of screenshots that are known to be correct.

- **Extensible automation**: Since monkeyrunner is an API toolkit, you can develop an entire system of Python-based modules and programs to control Android devices. Besides using the monkeyrunner API itself, you can use the standard Python OS and subprocess modules to call Android tools such as Android Debug Bridge. You can also add your own classes to the monkeyrunner API. This is described in more detail in the online documentation under Extending monkeyrunner with plugins.

Getting test screenshots

Currently, one of the most evident uses of monkeyrunner is getting screenshots of the application under test to be further analyzed or compared.

These screenshots can be obtained with the help of the following steps:

1. Import the required modules.
2. Create the connection with the device.
3. Check whether the device is connected.
4. Start the activity.
5. Add some delay for the activity start up.
6. Type 'hello'.
7. Add some delay to allow for the events to be processed.
8. Obtain the screenshots.
9. Save it to a file.
10. Press **BACK** to exit the Activity.

The following is the code for the script needed to perform the preceding steps:

```
#! /usr/bin/env monkeyrunner

import sys

# Imports the monkeyrunner modules used by this program
from com.android.monkeyrunner import MonkeyRunner, MonkeyDevice,
MonkeyImage
```

```
# Connects to the current device, returning a MonkeyDevice object
device = MonkeyRunner.waitForConnection()

if not device:
    print >> sys.stderr, "Couldn't" "get connection"
    sys.exit(1)

device.startActivity(component='com'.blundell.tut/.MonkeyActivity')

MonkeyRunner.sleep(3.0)

device.type("hello")

# Takes a screenshot
MonkeyRunner.sleep(3.0)
result = device.takeSnapshot()

# Writes the screenshot to a file
result.writeToFile('/tmp/device.png')

device.press('KEYCODE_BACK', 'DOWN'_AND_UP')
```

Once this script runs, you will find the screenshot of the activity in /tmp/device.png.

Record and playback

If you need something simpler, there is no need to manually create these scripts. To simplify the process, the monkey_recorder.py script, which is included in the Android source repository in the SDK project (http://goo.gl/6Qv0z0), can be used to record event descriptions that are later interpreted by another script called monkey_playback.py.

Run `monkey_recorder.py` from the command line, and you will be presented with this UI:

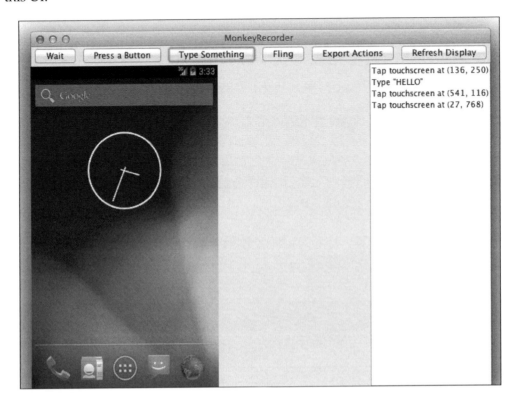

This interface has a toolbar with buttons to insert different commands in the recorded script:

Button	Description
Wait	This denotes how many seconds to wait. This number is requested by a dialog box.
Press a Button	This sends the **MENU, HOME, RECENTS,** and **SEARCH** buttons. Press the **Down** or **Up** event.
Type Something	This sends a string.
Fling	This sends a fling event in the specified direction, distance, and number of steps.
Export Actions	This saves the script.
Refresh Display	This refreshes the copy of the screenshot that is displayed.

Once the script is completed, save it, let's say as `script.mr`, and then, you can re-run it by using this command line:

```
$ monkey_playback.py script.mr
```

Now, all the events will be replayed.

Summary

In this chapter, we covered all the alternatives we had to expose our application and its tests to a wide range of conditions and configurations, ranging from different screen sizes, the availability of devices such as cameras or keyboards, to simulating real-life network conditions to detect problems in our application.

We also analyzed all of the options we have in order to be able to control emulators remotely when they are detached from its window. This prepares the foundation of doing test first development, and we will come back to this topic in *Chapter 6, Practicing Test-driven Development*.

We discussed the speed of the AVD and saw how we can improve this, as well as looked at emulator choices in GenyMotion and HAXM. Finally, some scripting alternatives were introduced, and examples to get you started were provided.

In the next chapter, we will discover continuous integration—a way of working that relies on the ability to automatically run all the test suites and configure, start, and stop emulators in order to automate the complete build process.

5
Discovering Continuous Integration

Continuous integration is one agile technique for software engineering that aims to improve software quality and reduce the time taken to integrate changes by continuously applying integration and testing frequently, as opposed to the more traditional approach of integrating and testing at the end of the development cycle.

Continuous integration has received a broad adoption, and a proliferation of commercial tools and open source projects is a clear demonstration of its success. That is not very difficult to understand, as anybody who during their professional career has participated in a software development project using a traditional approach is very likely to have experienced the so-called *integration hell*, where the time it takes to integrate the changes exceeds the time it took to make the changes. Does this remind you of anything?On the contrary, continuous integration is the practice of integrating changes frequently and in small steps. These steps are negligible and, if an error is noticed, it is so small that it can be fixed immediately. The most common practice is to trigger the build process after every commit to the source code repository.

This practice also implies other requirements, beside the source code being maintained by a version control system (VCS):

- Builds should be automated by running a single command. This feature has been supported for a very long time by tools such as `make` and `ant`, and more recently by `maven` and `gradle`.
- Builds should be self-testing to confirm that the newly built software meets the expectations of the developers.
- Build artifacts and results of the tests should be easy to find and view.

When we write tests for our Android projects, we would like to take advantage of continuous integration. To achieve this, we want to create a model that coexists with the traditional IDE environment and Android build tools, so we can run and install our app no matter the environment such as CI box, IDE or manually.

In this chapter, we are going to discuss:

- Automating the build process
- Introducing version control systems to the process
- Continuous integration with Jenkins
- Automating tests

After this chapter, you will be able to apply continuous integration to your own project no matter its size, whether it is a medium or large software project employing dozens of developers or it is just you programming solo.

> The original article on continuous integration was written by Martin Fowler back in 2000 (`http://www.martinfowler.com/articles/continuousIntegration.html`), and describes the experience of putting together continuous integration on a large software project.

Building Android applications manually using Gradle

If we aim to incorporate **continuous integration** into our development process, the first step will be to build Android applications manually, as we can combine an integration machine with the manual building technique to automate the procedure.

In doing this, we intend to keep our project compatible with the IDE and command-line building process, and this is what we are going to do. Automated building is a great advantage and speeds up the development process by building and eventually showing the errors that may exist in your project immediately. When editing resources or other files that generate intermediate classes, a CI is an invaluable tool; otherwise, some simple errors would be discovered too late in the building process. Following the mantra of fail often, fail fast is a recommended practice.

Fortunately, Android supports manual building with the existing tools and not much effort is needed to merge manual IDE builds and automatic CI builds in the same project. In such cases, building manually inside your IDE with Gradle is supported. However, other options such as Ant exist too that are no longer supported by default, and Maven or Make that are not supported out of the box.

Gradle is build automation evolved. Gradle combines the power and flexibility of Ant with the dependency management and conventions of Maven into a more effective way to build.

More information can be found at its home page, http://gradle.org/.

At the time of writing, projects based on Android Gradle require at least Gradle 2.2 or newer versions.

It is worth noting here that the entire Android open source project is not built by Gradle but built by an incredibly complex structure of make files, and this method is used even to build the applications that are included by the platform such as Calculator, Contacts, Settings, and so on.

When creating a new project with Android Studio, the template project will already be being built with Gradle. This means you can already build the project manually from the command line. Executing ./gradlew tasks from the base of your project will give you a full list of tasks that can be run. The most commonly used tasks are as shown in the following table:

Target	Description
build	Assembles and tests this project
clean	Deletes the build directory
tasks	Displays the tasks runnable from root project x (some of the displayed tasks may belong to subprojects)
installDebug	Installs the Debug build
installDebugTest	Installs the Test build for the Debug build
connectedAndroidTest	Installs and runs the tests for Build debug on connected devices
uninstallDebug	Uninstalls the Debug build

The commands prefixed with ./gradlew use an installation of Gradle that is actually shipped inside your project source code. This is known as the *gradle wrapper*. Therefore, you do not need Gradle installed on your local machine! However, if you do have Gradle installed locally, all commands using the wrapper can be replaced with ./gradle. If there are several devices or emulators connected to the build machine, these commands will run/install on them all. This is great for our CI setup, meaning we can run our tests on all the provided devices so that we can handle a number of configurations and Android versions. If you do want to install on just one for some other reason, this is possible through the Device Providers API but is out of the scope of this book. I encourage you to read more at www.tools.android.com and also check out the wide range of Gradle plugins available to help you with this.

Now we can run this command to install our application:

```
$ ./gradlew installDebug
```

This is the start and end of the output generated:

```
Configuring > 3/3 projects

...

:app:assembleDebug

:app:installDebug

Installing APK 'app'-debug.'apk' on 'emulator-5554'Installing APK 'app'-
debug.'apk'on 'Samsung'Galaxy 'S4'

Installed on 2 devices.


BUILD SUCCESSFUL

Total time: 11.011 secs
```

Running the preceding command mentioned, the following steps are executed:

- Compilation of the sources, including resource, AIDL, and Java files
- Conversion of the compiled files into the native Android format
- Package creation and signing
- Installation onto the given device or emulator

Once we have the APK installed, and because we are now doing everything from the command line, we can even start an Activity such as `EspressoActivity`. Using the `am start` command and an Intent using the `MAIN` action and the Activity we are interested to launch as the component, we can create a command line as follows:

```
adb -s emulator-5554 shell am start -a android.intent.action.MAIN -n com.
blundell.tut/.EspressoActivity
```

The Activity is started as you can verify in the emulator. Now the next thing to do would be to install the test project for our application, and then use the command line to run these tests (as discussed in previous chapters). Finally, when they are completed, we should uninstall the application. If you read the command list carefully, you may have noticed that luckily this has been done for us with the `connectedAndroidTest` Gradle task.

After running the command, we will obtain the tests results. If they pass, the output is simply as follows:

```
:app:connectedAndroidTest

BUILD SUCCESSFUL

Total time: 9.812 secs
```

However if they fail, the output is more detailed and a link to the file where you can see the full stack trace and the reasons why each test failed is presented:

```
:app:connectedAndroidTest

com.blundell.tut.ExampleEspressoTest > testClickingButtonShowsImage[emula
tor-5554]FAILED

android.view.ViewRootImpl$CalledFromWrongThreadException: Only the
original thread that created a view hierarchy can touch its views.

   at android.view.ViewRootImpl.checkThread(ViewRootImpl.java:6024)

FAILURE: Build failed with an exception.

* What went wrong:

Execution failed for task ':app:connectedAndroidTest.

> There were failing tests. See the report at: file:///
AndroidApplicationTestingGuide/app/build/outputs/reports/androidTests/
connected/index.html

...

BUILD FAILED

Total time: 15.532 secs
```

We have done everything from the command line by just invoking some simple commands, which is what we were looking for in order to feed this into a continuous integration process.

Git – the fast version control system

Git is a free and open source, distributed version control system designed to handle everything from small to very large projects with speed and efficiency. It is very simple to set up so I strongly recommend its use even for personal projects. There is no project simple enough that could not benefit from the application of this tool. You can find information and downloads at http://git-scm.com/.

A version control system or **VCS** (also known as source code management or **SCM**) is an unavoidable element for development projects where more than one developer is involved and the best practice even if coding solo. Furthermore, even though it is possible to apply continuous integration with no VCS in place (as a VCS is not a requisite of CI), it is not a reasonable or recommended practice to avoid it.

Other and probably more traditional (see legacy), options exist in the VCS arena such as Subversion or CVS, which you are free to use if you feel more comfortable. Otherwise, Git is used extensively by the Android project to host Google's own code and examples so it is worth investing some time to at least understand the basics.

Having said that and remembering that this is a very broad subject to justify a book in itself (and certainly there are some good books about it), we are discussing here the most basic topics and supplying examples to get you started if you haven't embraced this practice yet.

Creating a local Git repository

These are the simplest possible commands to create a local repository and populate it with the initial source code for our projects. In this case we are again using the AndroidApplicationTestingGuide project created and used in previous chapters. We copy the code we used in the previous section, where we built manually:

```
$ mkdir AndroidApplicationTestingGuide
$ cd AndroidApplicationTestingGuide
$ git init
$ cp -a <path/to/original>/AndroidApplicationTestingGuide/
$ gradlew clean
$ rm local.properties
$ git add .
$ git commit -m "Initial commit"
```

We create the new project directory, initialize the Git repository, copy the initial content, clean and delete our previous autogenerated files, remove the `local.properties` file, add everything to the repository, and commit.

> The `local.properties` file must never be checked in a version control system as it contains information specific to your local configuration. You might also want to look at creating a `.gitignore` file. This file allows you to define what files are not checked in (such as auto-generated files). An example of the `.gitignore` file can be found at `https://github.com/github/gitignore`.

At this point, we have our project repository containing the initial source code for our application and all of its tests. We haven't altered the structure so the project is still compatible with our IDE and Gradle for when we continue developing, locally building, and continuously integrating.

The next step is to have our project built and tested automatically every time we commit a change to the source code.

Continuous integration with Jenkins

Jenkins is an open source, extensible continuous integration server that has the ability to build and test software projects or monitor the execution of external jobs. Jenkins is easy to install and configure, and is thus widely used. That makes it ideal as an example to learn continuous integration.

Installing and configuring Jenkins

We mentioned easy installation as one of the advantages of Jenkins and installation could not be any easier. Download the native package for the operating system of your choice from `http://jenkins-ci.org/`. There are native packages for all major server and desktop operating systems. In the following examples, we will be using version 1.592. We will run the `.war` file after downloading it, since it does not require administrative privileges to do so.

Once finished, copy the war into a selected directory, `~/jenkins`, and then run the following command:

```
$ java -jar ~/jenkins/jenkins-1.592.war
```

This expands and starts Jenkins.

The default configuration uses port `8080` as the HTTP listener port, so pointing your browser of choice to `http://localhost:8080` should present you with the Jenkins home page. You can verify and change Jenkins' operating parameter if required, by accessing the **Manage Jenkins** screen. We should add to this configuration the plugins needed for Git integration, building with Gradle, checking test results, and support for Android emulator during builds. These plugins are named **Git plugin**, **Gradle plugin**, **JUnit plugin**, and **Android Emulator plugin**, respectively.

This following screenshot displays the information you can obtain about the plugins following the link available on the Jenkins plugin administration page:

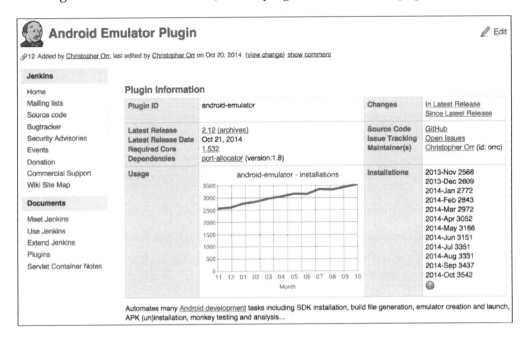

After installing and restarting Jenkins, these plugins will be available for use. Our next step is to create the jobs necessary to build the projects.

Creating the jobs

Let's start by creating the AndroidApplicationTestingGuide job using **New Item** on the Jenkins home page. Name it after the project. Different kinds of jobs can be created; in this case, we select **Freestyle project**, allowing you to connect any SCM with any build system.

After clicking on the **OK** button, you will be presented with the specific job options, which are described in the following table. This is at the top of the job properties' page as follows:

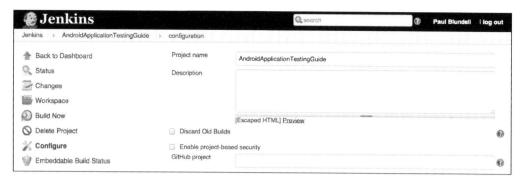

All of the options in the **New Item** screen have a help text associated, so here we are only explaining the ones we enter:

Option	Description
Project name	The name given to the project.
Description	Optional description.
Discard Old Builds	This helps you save on disk consumption by managing how long to keep records of the builds (such as console output, build artifacts, and so on).
This build is parameterized	This allows you to configure parameters that are passed to the build process to create parameterized builds, for instance, using $ANDROID_HOME instead of hardcoding a path.
Source Code Management

Also known as VCS, where is the source code for the project? In this case, we use Git and a repository where the URL is the absolute path of the repository we created earlier. For example, /git-repo/AndroidApplication TestingGuide. | |

Option	Description
Build Triggers	How this project is automatically built. In this case, we want every change in the source code to trigger the automatic build, so we select **Poll SCM**.
	The other option is to use **Build periodically**. This feature is primarily to use Jenkins as a `cron` replacement, and it is not ideal to continuously build software projects. When people first start continuous integration, they are often so used to the idea of regularly scheduled builds such as nightly/weekly that they use this feature. However, the point of continuous integration is to start a build as soon as a change is made, to provide a quick feedback to the change.
	This option can be used for longer running builds like test suites that perhaps test performance when the build runs for 1 hour for example (configure it to run at midnight). It also can be used to release new versions, nightly, or weekly.
Schedule	This field follows the syntax of `Cron` (with minor differences). Specifically, each line consists of five fields separated by TAB or whitespace:
	`MINUTE HOUR DOM MONTH DOW.`
	For example, if we want to poll continuously at 30 minutes past the hour, specify:
	`30 * * * *`
	Check the documentation for a complete explanation of all the options.
Build environment	This option lets you specify different options for the build environment and for the Android emulator that may run during the build.
Build	This option describes the build steps. We select **Invoke Gradle script** as we reproduce the steps we did before to manually build and test the project.
	We will select **Use Gradle Wrapper** so that our project doesn't rely on the CI boxes built in the Gradle version.
	Then, in the **Tasks** box, we want to write `clean connectedAndroidTest`.

Option	Description
Post build actions	These are a series of actions we can do after the build is done. We are interested in saving the APKs so we enable **Archive the artifacts** and then define the path for them as **Files to archive**; in this precise case, it is `**/*-debug.apk`.
Save	Saves the changes we just made and completes the build job creation.

Now that our CI build is set up, there are following two options:

- You can force a build using **Build Now**
- Or introduce some changes to the source code, push with Git, and wait for them to be detected by our polling strategy

Either way, we will get our project built and our artifacts ready to be used for other purposes, such as dependency projects or QA. Unfortunately, if you did run the CI build, it would fail spectacularly as there are no devices attached. Your choices are, attach a real device or use the Android Emulator plugin that we just installed. Let's use the plugin. From Jenkins, go to the job we just created and click on **Configure**.

Option	Description
Build environment	Our intention is to install and run the tests on an emulator. So for our build environment, we use the facilities provided by the **Android Emulator Plugin**. This comes in handy if you wish to automatically start an Android emulator of your choice before the build steps execute, with the emulator being stopped after the building is complete.
	You can choose to start a predefined, existing Android emulator instance (AVD).
	Alternatively, the plugin can automatically create a new emulator on the build slave with properties you specify here.
	In any case, the `logcat` output will automatically be captured and archived.
	Select **Run emulator with properties**.
	Then, select **4.4** for the **Android OS version**, **320** DPI for the **Screen density** and **WQVGA** for **Screen resolution**.
	Feel free to experiment and select the options that better suit your needs.
Common emulator options	We would like to **Reset emulator state at start-up** to wipe user data and disable **Show emulator window**, so the emulator window is not displayed.

After configuring and building this project, we have the APK installed on the target emulator and the tests are running.

Obtaining Android test results

Once the tests are run, the results are saved as XML files inside the project's build folder at `/AndroidApplicationTestingGuides/app/build/outputs/androidTest-results/connected/`.

They are no good to us there. It would be nice if we could read the results of our tests in Jenkins and have them displayed in a nice HTML format; another Jenkins plugin to the rescue. JUnit Plugin enables a post build action that asks you where your JUnit reports are stored and will then retrieve them for easy viewing in the project screen of Jenkins as test results. In this scenario, we use the Post-build Actions also in the job configuration's page.

Having done all of the steps previously described, only forcing a build is left to see the results. Option	Description
Publish JUnit test result report	When this option is configured, the JUnit plugin on Jenkins can provide useful information about test results, such as historical test result trends, a web UI to view test reports, tracking failures, and so on.
	It requires a regex to look up the JUnit result files. I would recommend `**/TEST*.xml`. This regex should match all JUnit test results, including those of the Android connected tests; praise in research here goes to Adam Brown. If you change the regex, be sure not to include any non-report files into this pattern.
	Once a few builds have run with test results, you should start seeing some trend charts displaying the evolution of tests.

Click on **Build Now** and after a few moments, you will see your test results and statistics displayed in a similar way as the following screenshot depicts:

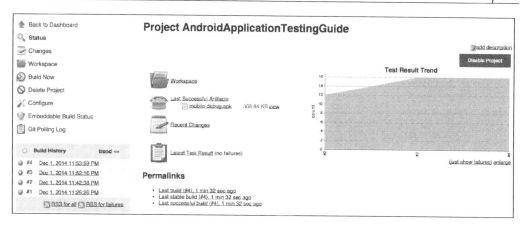

From here, we can easily understand our project status. Clicking on **Latest Test Result** shows you how many tests failed and why. You can search through the failed tests and can also find the extensive **Error message** and **Stack trace** options.

It is also really helpful to understand the evolution of a project through the evaluation of different trends and Jenkins is able to provide such information. Every project presents the current trends using weather-like icons from sunny, when the health of the project increases by 80 percent, and to thunderstorm when the health lies below 20 percent. In addition, for every project, the evolution of the trend of the tests success versus failure ratio is displayed in a chart. A failing test chart is reproduced here:

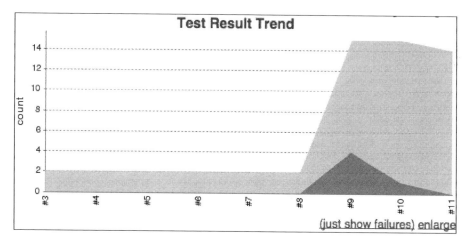

In this case, we can see how at build 9, four tests where broken, three where fixed in build 10, and the final one in build 11.

To see how a project status changes by forcing a failure, let's add a failing test such as the following. Don't forget to push your commit to trigger the CI build as follows:

```
public final void testForceFailure() {
  fail("fail test is fail");
}
```

Yet another very interesting feature that is worth mentioning is the ability of Jenkins to keep and display the timeline and build the time trend, as shown in the following screenshot:

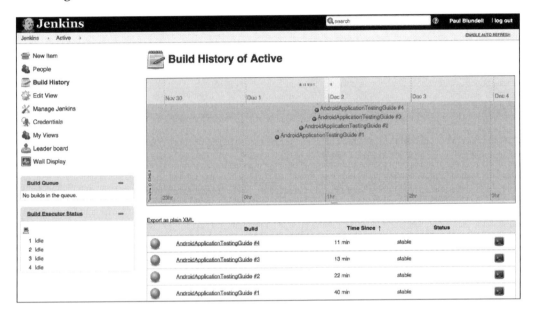

This page presents the build history with links to every particular build that you can follow to see the details. Now we have less to be worried about and every time somebody in the development team commits changes to the repository, we know that these changes will be immediately integrated and the whole project will be built and tested. If we further configure Jenkins, we can even receive the status by e-mail. To achieve this, enable **E-mail Notification** in the job configuration page and enter the desired **Recipients**.

Summary

This chapter introduced continuous integration in practice providing valuable information to start applying it soon to your projects no matter what their size, whether you are developing solo or a part of a big company team.

The techniques presented focus on the particularities of Android projects maintaining and supporting widely used development tools such as Android Studio and the Android Gradle plugin.

We introduced real-world examples with real-world tools available from the vast open source arsenal. We employed Gradle to automate the building process, Git to create a simple version control system repository to store our source code and manage the changes, and finally, installed and configured Jenkins as the continuous integration of choice.

Within Jenkins, we detailed the creation of jobs to automate the creation of our Android application and its tests, and we emphasized the relationship between the continuous integration box and its devices/emulators.

Finally, we became aware of the Android-connected tests results and implemented a strategy to obtain an attractive interface to monitor the running of tests, their results, and the existing trends.

The next chapter takes us through the road of Test-driven Development; you'll finally start to understand why I keep talking about the temperature in all the examples so far with a real-world project. Thus, having a continuous integration setup is perfect to empower us to write great code and have faith in our CI built APKs being ready to release.

6
Practicing Test-driven Development

This chapter introduces the **Test-driven Development** (TDD) discipline. We will start with TDD practices in the general sense, and later on move to the concepts and techniques more closely related to the Android platform.

This is a code-intensive chapter, so be prepared to type as you read, which would help you get the most out of the examples provided.

In this chapter, we will learn the following topics:

- Introducing and explaining Test-driven Development
- Analyzing its advantages
- Introducing a real-life example
- Understanding project requirements by writing tests
- Evolving through the project by applying TDD
- Getting an application that fully complies with the requirements

Getting started with TDD

Briefly, Test-driven Development is the strategy of writing tests in parallel with the development process. These test cases are written in advance of the code that is supposed to satisfy them.

A single test is written, and then the code needed to satisfy the compilation of this test is written, then the behavior that the test decrees should exist is written. We continue writing tests and implementation until the full set of desired behaviors is checked by the tests.

This contrasts with other approaches to the development process, where the tests are written at the end when all the coding has been done.

Writing the tests in advance of the code that satisfies them has the following advantages:

- Tests get written one way or another, while if the tests are left till the end it is highly probable that they will never be written
- Developers take more responsibility for the quality of their work, when having to consider the tests as they code

Design decisions are taken in smaller steps and afterwards the code satisfying the tests is improved by refactoring. Remember, this is while having the tests running, so that there are no regressions in expected behavior.

Test-driven Development is often explained in a diagram like the following, to help us understand the process:

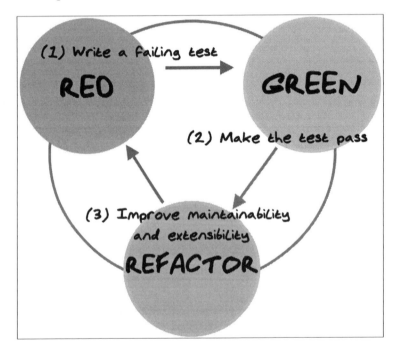

The following sections expand on the individual actions associated with the TDD, red, green, refactor cycle.

Writing a test case

We start our development process with writing a test case. This apparently is a simple process that will put some machinery to work inside our heads. After all, it is not possible to write some code, test it or not, if we don't have a clear understanding of the problem domain, and its details. Usually, this step will get you face to face with the aspects of the problem you don't understand, and you need to grasp these if you want to model and write the code.

Running all tests

Once the test is written the next step is to run it, along with all other tests we have written so far. Here, the importance of an IDE with built-in support of the testing environment is perhaps more evident than in other situations, cutting the development time by a good fraction. It is expected that, firstly, our newly written test fails as we still haven't written any code.

To be able to complete our test, we write additional code and take design decisions. The additional code written is the minimum possible to get our test to compile. Consider here, that not compiling is failing.

When we get the test to compile and run, and if the test fails, then we try to write the minimum amount of code necessary to make the test succeed. This may sound awkward at this point, but the following code example in this chapter will help you understand the process.

Optionally, instead of running all tests again you can just run the newly added tests first, to save some time as sometimes running the tests on the emulator could be rather slow. Then run the whole test suite to verify that everything is still working properly. We don't want to add a new feature by breaking any features already existing in our code.

Refactoring the code

When the test succeeds, we refactor the code added to keep it tidy, clean, and the minimal needed for a maintainable and extensible application.

We run all the tests again, to verify that our refactoring has not broken anything, and if the tests are again satisfied and no more refactoring is needed, we finish our task.

Running the tests after refactoring is an incredible safety net that has been put in place by this methodology. If we made a mistake refactoring an algorithm, extracting variables, introducing parameters, changing signatures, or whatever the refactoring mechanism, this testing infrastructure will detect the problem. Furthermore, if some refactoring or optimization could not be valid for every possible case, we can verify it for every case used by the application expressing this as a test case.

Advantages of TDD

Personally, the main advantage I've seen so far is that it quickly focuses you on your programming goal, and it is harder to get distracted or eager, and implement options in your software that will never be used (sometimes known as gold plating). This implementation of unneeded features is a waste of your precious development time and as you may already know, judiciously administering these resources may be the difference between successfully reaching the end of the project or not.

The other advantage is that you always have a safety net for your changes. Every time you change a piece of code, you can be absolutely sure that other parts of the system are not affected, as long as there are tests verifying that the conditions haven't changed.

Don't forget, TDD cannot be indiscriminately applied to any project. I think that, as well as any other technique; you should use your judgment and expertise to recognize where it can be applied and where not. Always remember: *there are no silver bullets*.

Understanding the requirements

To be able to write a test about any subject, we should first understand the subject under test, this means breaking apart the requirement you are attempting to implement.

We mentioned that one of the advantages is that you focus upon a goal quickly, instead of revolving around the requirements as a big, unconquerable whole.

Translating requirements into tests and cross referencing them is perhaps the best way to understand the requirements, and to be sure that there is always an implementation and verification for all of them. Also, when the requirements change (something that is very frequent in software development projects), we can change the tests verifying these requirements, and then change the implementation to be sure that everything was correctly understood and mapped to the code.

Creating a sample project – the temperature converter

You might have guessed it from some of the code snippets so far, that our TDD examples will revolve around an extremely simple Android sample project. It doesn't try to show all the fancy Android features, but focuses on testing and gradually building the application from the test, applying the concepts learned before.

Let's pretend that we have received a list of requirements to develop an Android temperature converter application. Though oversimplified, we will be following the steps you normally would, to develop such an application. However, in this case we will introduce the Test-driven Development techniques in the process.

List of requirements

Usually (let's be honest), the list of requirements are very vague, and there are a high number of details not fully covered.

As an example, let's pretend that we receive this list:

- The application converts temperatures from Celsius to Fahrenheit and vice-versa
- The user interface presents two fields to enter the temperatures; one for Celsius the other for Fahrenheit
- When a temperature is entered in one field, the other one is automatically updated with the conversion
- If there are errors, they should be displayed to the user, possibly using the same fields
- Some space in the user interface should be reserved for the on-screen keyboard, to ease the application operation when several conversions are entered
- Entry fields should start empty
- Values entered are decimal values with two digits after the point
- Digits are right aligned
- Last entered values should be retained even after the application is paused

User interface concept design

Let's assume that we receive this conceptual user interface design from the
user interface design team (I apologize right now to all designers for my lack of
imagination and skill):

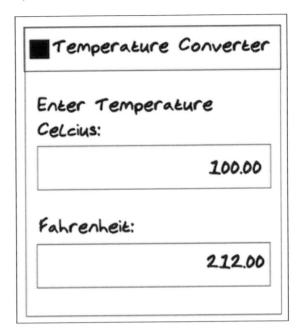

Creating the project

Our first step is to create the project. Now, since we have done this for five chapters
already I don't think I need to give you a step-by-step guide. Just run through the
Android Studio new project wizard, and select an Android mobile project with your
package name, plus other boilerplate, and no Activity template. Android Studio
will automatically create you an example `AndroidApplicationTestCase`. Bear in
mind, if you get stuck, you can refer to the code accompaniment for this book. When
created, it should look something like this:

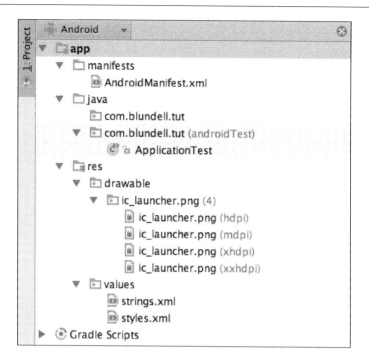

Now let's quickly create a new Activity called `TemperatureConverterActivity` (we didn't use the template generator, because it adds loads of code that is not needed right now), don't forget to add the Activity to your `AndroidManifest` file. Fanatic TDD'ers might be shaking their fist right now, as really you should make this Activity only when needed in your tests, but I'm trying to guide you with some familiarity at the same time.

Creating a Java module

On top of this template project, we want to add another module of code. This will be a Java-only module and will act as a dependency or library, if you will, for our main Android module.

The idea here is two-fold. First, it allows you to separate code that is Java only, and does not have a dependency on Android, in a big project this can be your core domain; the business logic that runs your app, and it is important that you modularize this, so you can work on it without having to think about Android as well.

Secondly, having a Java-only module as we've said before, allows you to call on the vast history of Java as an established programming language when it comes to testing. Testing of the Java module is fast, simple, and easy. You can write JUnit tests for the JVM and have them running in milliseconds (which we will do!).

From Android Studio, navigate to **File | New Module,** this gives you the **Create new module** dialog. Under **More Modules**, select **Java Library,** and hit **Next**. Name your library `core`, and ensure the package name is the same as your Android application, and press on **Finish**. The last screen should have looked something like this:

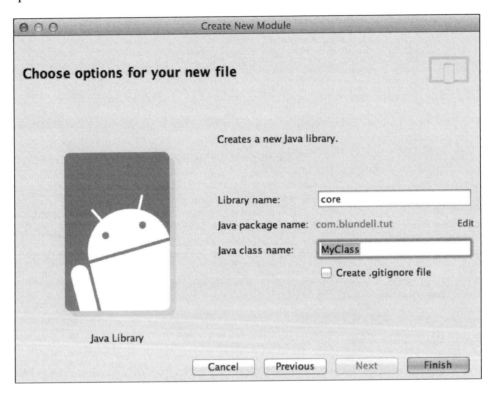

Once created, you need to add the one-way dependency from your Android `:app` module to the `:core` module. Within, `/app/build.gradle`, add the dependency on core:

```
dependencies {
    compile fileTree(dir: 'libs', include: ['*.jar'])
    compile 'com.android.support:appcompat-v7:21.0.2'

    compile project(':core')
}
```

This allows us to reference files from our core module inside of our Android application.

Creating the TemperatureConverterActivityTests class

Proceed with creating the first test by selecting the main test package name, `com.blundell.tut`. This is under `src/androidTest/Java` in the AndroidStudio project view, or under `app/java/(androidTest)` in the AndroidStudio Android view. Then right-click here, and select **New | Java Class**, call it, `TemperatureConverterActivityTests`.

Once the class is created, we need to go about turning it into a test class. We should select our superclass depending on what and how we are going to test. In *Chapter 2, Understanding Testing with the Android SDK*, we reviewed the available alternatives. Use it as a reference when you try to decide what superclass to use.

In this particular case, we are testing a single Activity and using the system infrastructure, therefore, we should use `ActivityInstrumentationTestCase2`. Also note that as `ActivityInstrumentationTestCase2` is a generic class, we need the template parameter as well. This is the Activity under test, which in our case, is `TemperatureConverterActivity`.

We now notice that our class has some errors we need to fix before running. Otherwise the errors will prevent the test from running.

The problem we need to fix has been described before in *Chapter 2, Understanding Testing with the Android SDK*, under the *The no-argument constructor* section. As this pattern dictates, we need to implement:

```java
public TemperatureConverterActivityTests() {
  this("TemperatureConverterActivityTests");
}

public TemperatureConverterActivityTests(String name) {
  super(TemperatureConverterActivity.class);
  setName(name);
}
```

So far we have performed the following steps:

- We added the no argument constructor `TemperatureConverterActivityTests()`. From this constructor, we invoke the constructor that takes a name as a parameter.

- Finally, in this given name constructor, we invoke the super constructor and set the name.

To verify that everything has been set up and is in place, you may run the tests by right clicking on the class, and selecting **Run | The Name of the Test Class**. There are no tests to run yet, but at least we can verify that the infrastructure supporting our tests is already in place. It should fail with a **No tests** found warning. Here is how to run the test class, in case you missed it:

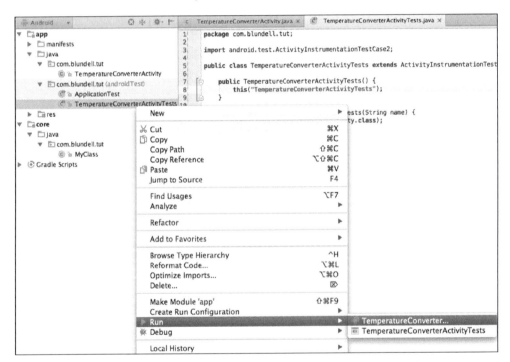

Creating the fixture

We can start creating our test fixture by populating the `setup()` method with the elements we need in our tests. Almost unavoidable, in this case, is the use of the Activity under test, so let's prepare for the situation and add it to the fixture:

```
@Override
public void setUp() throws Exception {
```

```
        super.setUp();
        activity = getActivity();
    }
```

After introducing the previous code, create the `activity` field using AndroidStudio's refactoring tools to save you time. (*F2* for next error, *Alt + Enter* for quick fix, *Enter* again to create field, *Enter* again to confirm the fields type, done!)

The `ActivityInstrumentationTestCase2.getActivity()` method has a side effect. If the Activity under test is not running, it will be started. This may change the intention of a test if we use `getActivity()` as a simple accessor several times in a test, and for some reason the Activity finishes or crashes before test completion. We will be inadvertently restarting the Activity, that is why in our tests we discourage the use of `getActivity()` in favor of having it in the fixture, so that we are implicitly restarting the activity for every test.

Creating the user interface

Back to our Test-driven Development track, we see from our concise list of requirements that there are two entries for Celsius and Fahrenheit temperatures, respectively. So let's add them to our test fixture.

They don't exist yet, and we haven't even started designing the user interface layout, but we know that there should be two entries like these for sure.

This is the code you should add to the `setUp()` method:

```
celsiusInput = (EditText)
    activity.findViewById(R.id.converter_celsius_input);
fahrenheitInput = (EditText)
    activity.findViewById(R.id.converter_fahrenheit_input);
```

There are some important things to notice:

- We choose the names `converter_celsius_input` because, `converter_` is the location of this field (in the `TemperatorConverter` Activity) `celsius_` is what the field represents, and finally input is how the fields behave

- We define the fields for our fixture using `EditText`

- We use the previously created Activity to find the Views by ID

- We use the `R` class for the main project even though these IDs do not exist

Testing the existence of the user interface components

Once we have added them to the `setUp()` method, as indicated in the previous section, we can write our first test and check the views existence:

```
public final void testHasInputFields() {
  assertNotNull(celsiusInput);
  assertNotNull(fahrenheitInput);
}
```

We are not able to run the tests yet because we must fix some compilation problems first. We should fix the missing IDs in the R class.

Having created our test fixture that references elements and IDs in the user interface that we don't have yet, it's mandated by the Test-driven Development paradigm that we add the needed code to satisfy our tests. The first thing we should do is get the test to compile, so if we have some tests testing unimplemented features, they will fail.

Getting the IDs defined

Our first stop would be to have the IDs for the user interface elements defined in the R class, so the errors generated by referencing undefined constants `R.id.converter_celsius_input` and `R.id.converter_fahrenheit_input` go away.

You, as an experienced Android developer, will know how to do it. I'll give you a refresher anyway. Create an `activity_temperature_converter.xml` layout in the layout editor, and add the required user interface components to get something that resembles the design previously introduced in the *User Interface concept design* section, as shown in the following code:

```
<?xml version="1.0" encoding="utf-8"?>
<LinearLayout xmlns:android="http://schemas.android.com/apk/res/
android"
  android:layout_width="match_parent"
  android:layout_height="match_parent"
  android:orientation="vertical">


  <TextView
    android:layout_width="match_parent"
    android:layout_height="wrap_content"
    android:layout_marginBottom="@dimen/margin"
```

```
    android:text="@string/message" />

  <<TextView
    android:id="@+id/converter_celsius_label"
    android:layout_width="wrap_content"
    android:layout_height="wrap_content"
    android:layout_marginStart="@dimen/margin"
    android:text="@string/celsius" />

  <EditText
    android:id="@+id/converter_celsius_input"
    android:layout_width="wrap_content"
    android:layout_height="wrap_content"
    android:layout_margin="@dimen/margin"  />

  <TextView
    android:id="@+id/converter_fahrenheit_label"
    android:layout_width="wrap_content"
    android:layout_height="wrap_content"
    android:layout_marginStart="@dimen/margin"
    android:text="@string/fahrenheit"  />

  <EditText
    android:id="@+id/converter_fahrenheit_input"
    android:layout_width="wrap_content"
    android:layout_height="wrap_content"
    android:layout_margin="@dimen/margin"  />
</LinearLayout>
```

Doing so, we get our tests to compile (don't forget to add the strings and dimensions), run the tests, do they pass? They shouldn't! You need to hook up your new activity layout (I bet you beat me to it):

```
public class TemperatureConverterActivity extends Activity {
    @Override
    protected void onCreate(Bundle savedInstanceState) {
        super.onCreate(savedInstanceState);
        setContentView(R.layout.activity_temperature_converter);
    }
}
```

Run the tests once more, and you should get the following result:

- The `testHasInputFields` test succeeded
- Everything is green now

The output of the test is seen as follows:

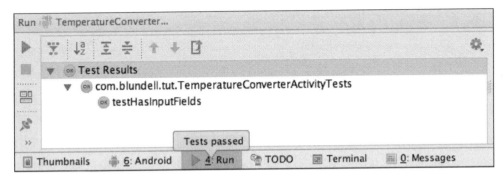

This clearly means that we are on track with applying TDD.

You may also have noticed that we added some decorative and non-functional items to our user interface that we are not testing (say padding), mainly to keep our example as simple as possible. In a real-case scenario, you may want to add tests for these elements too.

Translating requirements to tests

Tests have a double feature. They verify the correctness of our code but, sometimes, and more prominently in TDD, they help us understand the design and digest what we are implementing. To be able to create the tests, we need to understand the problem we are dealing with, and if we don't, we should at least have a rough outline of the problem to allow us to start to handle it.

Many times, the requirements behind the user interface are not clearly expressed, but you should be able to understand them from the wireframed UI design. If we pretend that this is the case, then we can grasp the design by writing our tests first.

Empty fields

From one of our requirements, we get: Entry fields should start empty.

To express this in a test, we can write the following:

```
public void testFieldsShouldStartEmpty() {
```

```
        assertEquals("", celsiusInput.getText().toString());
        assertEquals("", fahrenheitInput.getText().toString());
    }
```

Here, we simply compare the initial contents of the fields against the empty string.

This test passes straight away, great! Although a tenant of TDD always starts with a red test, you might want to do a quick sanity check, and add some text to the XML for `EditText` and run the tests, and when it goes red and green again when you remove the added text, you know your test is validating the behavior you expect (and it wasn't green as a side effect of something you did not expect). We successfully converted one requirement to a test, and validated it by obtaining the test results.

View properties

Identically, we can verify other properties of the Views composing our layout. Among other things, we can verify:

- Fields (appear on the screen as expected)
- Font sizes
- Margins
- Screen alignment

Let's start verifying that the fields are on the screen:

```
    public void testFieldsOnScreen() {
        View origin = activity.getWindow().getDecorView();

        assertOnScreen(origin, celsiusInput);
        assertOnScreen(origin, fahrenheitInput);
    }
```

As explained before, we use an assert from here: `ViewAsserts: assertOnScreen`.

 Static imports and how to make the most of them was explained in *Chapter 2, Understanding Testing with the Android SDK*. If you haven't done it before, now is the time.

The `assertOnScreen()` method needs an origin to start looking for the other Views. In this case, because we want to start from the top-most level, we use `getDecorView()`, which retrieves the top-level window view containing the standard window frame and decorations, with the client's content inside.

By running this test, we can ensure that the entry fields are on the screen, as the UI design dictates. In some way, we already knew that Views, with these specific IDs, existed. That is, we made the fixture compile by adding the Views to the main layout, but we were not sure they were appearing on the screen at all. So, nothing else is needed but the sole presence of this test, to ensure that the condition is not changed in the future. If we remove one of the fields for some reason, this test will tell us that it is missing, and not complying with the UI design.

Following with our list of requirements, we should test that the Views are aligned in the layout as we expect:

```
public void testAlignment() {
    assertLeftAligned(celsiusLabel, celsiusInput);
    assertLeftAligned(fahrenheitLabel, fahrenheitInput);
    assertLeftAligned(celsiusInput, fahrenheitInput);
    assertRightAligned(celsiusInput, fahrenheitInput);
}
```

We continue using asserts from `ViewAssert` — in this case, `assertLeftAligned` and `assertRightAligned`. These methods verify the alignment of the specified Views. To get this test running we have to add the two lookups for the label TextView's in the `setUp()` method:

```
celsiusLabel = (TextView)
  activity.findViewById(R.id.converter_celsius_label);
fahrenheitLabel = (TextView)
  activity.findViewById(R.id.converter_fahrenheit_label);
```

The `LinearLayout` class we are using by default arranges the fields in the way we are expecting them. Again, while we don't need to add anything to the layout, to satisfy the test, this will act as a guard condition.

Once we've verified that they are correctly aligned, we should verify that they are covering the whole screen width, as specified by the schematic drawing. In this example, it's sufficient to verify `LayoutParams` having the correct values:

```
public void testCelciusInputFieldCoversEntireScreen() {
  LayoutParams lp;
  int expected = LayoutParams.MATCH_PARENT;
  lp = celsiusInput.getLayoutParams();
  assertEquals("celsiusInput layout width is not MATCH_PARENT",
expected, lp.width);
  }

public void testFahrenheitInputFieldCoversEntireScreen() {
  LayoutParams lp;
```

```
    int expected = LayoutParams.MATCH_PARENT;
    lp = fahrenheitInput.getLayoutParams();
    assertEquals("fahrenheitInput layout width is not MATCH_PARENT",
expected, lp.width);
    }
```

We used a custom message to easily identify the problem, in case the test fails.

By running this test, we obtain the following message indicating that the test failed: **AssertionFailedError: celsiusInput layout width is not MATCH_PARENT expected:<-1> but was:<-2>**.

This leads us to the layout definition. We must change `layout_width` to be `match_parent` for the Celsius and Fahrenheit fields:

```
<EditText
    android:id="@+id/converter_celsius_input"
    android:layout_width="match_parent"
    android:layout_height="wrap_content"
    android:layout_margin="@dimen/margin"
    android:gravity="end|center_vertical" />
```

Same for Fahrenheit—after the change is done, we repeat the cycle, and by running the test again, we can verify that it is now successful.

Our method is starting to appear. We create the test to verify a condition described in the requirements. If it's not met, we change the cause of the problem, and running the tests again, we verify that the latest change solves the problem, and what is perhaps more important is that the change doesn't break the existing code.

Next, let's verify that the font sizes are defined as per our requirements:

```
public void testFontSizes() {
    float pixelSize = 24f;
    assertEquals(pixelSize, celsiusLabel.getTextSize());
    assertEquals(pixelSize, fahrenheitLabel.getTextSize());
}
```

Retrieving the font size used by the field is enough in this case.

The default font size is not 24px, so we need to add this to our layout. It's a good practice to add the corresponding dimension to a resource file, and then use it where it's needed in the layout. So, let's add `label_text_size` to `res/values/dimens.xml`, with a value of 24sp. Then reference it in the `Text size` property of the labels, `celsius_label` and `fahrenheit_label`.

Now, the test may pass or it may not, depending on the resolution of your device or emulator you are using. This is because we are asserting in the test, the pixel size, but we have declared in the dimens.xml, to use sp (scale independent pixels). Let's harden this test. To resolve this we could either convert our px to sp in the test class, or use the sp value in the test. I have chosen to use sp in the test, although you could argue for either:

```
public void testFontSizes() {
    float pixelSize = getFloatPixelSize(R.dimen.label_text_size);

    assertEquals(pixelSize, celsiusLabel.getTextSize());
    assertEquals(pixelSize, fahrenheitLabel.getTextSize());
}

private float getFloatPixelSize(int dimensionResourceId) {
    return getActivity().getResources()
            .getDimensionPixelSize(dimensionResourceId);
}
```

Finally, let's verify that margins are interpreted as described in the user interface design:

```
public void testCelsiusInputMargins() {
    LinearLayout.LayoutParams lp =
(LinearLayout.LayoutParams) celsiusInput.getLayoutParams();

    assertEquals(getIntPixelSize(R.dimen.margin), lp.leftMargin);
    assertEquals(getIntPixelSize(R.dimen.margin), lp.rightMargin);
}

public void testFahrenheitInputMargins() {
    LinearLayout.LayoutParams lp =
(LinearLayout.LayoutParams) fahrenheitInput.getLayoutParams();

    assertEquals(getIntPixelSize(R.dimen.margin), lp.leftMargin);
    assertEquals(getIntPixelSize(R.dimen.margin), lp.rightMargin);
}
```

This is a similar case as before (I've skipped the step of testing the raw pixel value). We need to add the margin to our layout. Let's add the margin dimension to the resource file, and then use it where it's needed in the layout. Set the margin dimension in res/values/dimens.xml to a value of 8dp. Then, reference it in the layout_margin_start property of both fields, celsius and fahrenheit, and also in the start margin of the labels.

The `helper` method to get the integer pixel size from a resource `dimen`, just wraps the `float` method already discussed:

```
private int getIntPixelSize(int dimensionResourceId) {
    return (int) getFloatPixelSize(dimensionResourceId);
}
```

One more thing that is left is to verify the justification (alignment) of the entered values. We will validate the input shortly, to allow only the permitted values, but for now let's just pay attention to the justification. The intention is to have values that are smaller than the whole field, justified to the right and vertically centered:

```
public void testCelsiusInputJustification() {
    int expectedGravity = Gravity.END | Gravity.CENTER_VERTICAL;
    int actual = celsiusInput.getGravity();
    String errorMessage = String.format(
"Expected 0x%02x but was 0x%02x", expectedGravity, actual);
    assertEquals(errorMessage, expectedGravity, actual);
}

public void testFahrenheitInputJustification() {
    int expectedGravity = Gravity.END | Gravity.CENTER_VERTICAL;
    int actual = fahrenheitInput.getGravity();
    String errorMessage = String.format(
"Expected 0x%02x but was 0x%02x", expectedGravity, actual);
    assertEquals(errorMessage, expectedGravity, actual);
}
```

Here, we verify the `gravity` values as usual. However, we are using a custom message to help us identify the values that could be wrong. As the `Gravity` class defines several constants whose values are better identified if expressed in hexadecimal, we are converting the values to this base in the message.

If this test is failing due to the default gravity used for the fields, then what is only left is to change it. Go to the layout definition and alter these `gravity` values, so that the test succeeds.

This is precisely what we need to add:

```
android:gravity="end|center_vertical"
```

Screen layout

We now want to verify that the requirement specifying that enough screen space should be reserved to display the keyboard, is actually fulfilled.

We can write a test like this:

```
public void testVirtualKeyboardSpaceReserved() {
        int expected = getIntPixelSize(R.dimen.keyboard_space);
        int actual = fahrenheitInput.getBottom();
String errorMessage =
    "Space not reserved, expected " + expected + " actual " + actual;
        assertTrue(errorMessage, actual <= expected);
    }
```

This verifies that the actual position of the last field in the screen, which is `fahrenheitInput`, is not lower than a suggested value.

We can run the tests again verifying that everything is green again. Run up your application, and you should have a complete user interface backed by tests, as shown in the following screenshot:

Adding functionality

The user interface is in place. Now, we can start adding some basic functionality. This functionality will include the code to handle the actual temperature conversion.

Temperature conversion

From the list of requirements, we can obtain this statement: When one temperature is entered in one field, the other one is automatically updated with the conversion.

Following our plan, we must implement this as a test to verify that the correct functionality is there. Our test would look something like this:

```
@UiThreadTest
public void testFahrenheitToCelsiusConversion() {
  celsiusInput.clear();
  fahrenheitInput.clear();
  fahrenheitInput.requestFocus();
  fahrenheitInput.setText("32.5");
  celsiusInput.requestFocus();
  double f = 32.5;
  double expectedC = TemperatureConverter.fahrenheitToCelsius(f);
  double actualC = celsiusInput.getNumber();
  double delta = Math.abs(expectedC - actualC);
  String msg = "" + f + "F -> " + expectedC + "C but was "
    + actualC + "C (delta " + delta + ")";
  assertTrue(msg, delta < 0.005);
}
```

Let's run through this step-by-step:

1. Firstly, as we already know, to interact with the UI changing its values we should run the test on the UI thread, and thus because we use `EditText.setText`, the test is annotated with `@UiThreadTest`.

2. Secondly, we are using a specialized class to replace `EditText` providing some convenience methods such as `clear()` and `setNumber()`. This will improve our application design.

3. Next, we invoke a converter, named `TemperatureConverter`, a utility class providing the different methods to convert between different temperature units, and using different types for the temperature values.

4. Finally, as we will be truncating the results to provide them in a suitable format presented in the user interface, we should compare against a delta to assert the value of the conversion.

Creating the test like this will force us to follow the planned path. Our first objective is to add the needed methods and code to get the test to compile, and then to satisfy the test's needs.

The EditNumber class

In our main package, not in the tests one (which is not the one under / androidTest/), we should create the EditNumber class extending EditText, as we need to extend its functionality. Once the class is created, we need to change the type of the fields in our test class member types:

```
public class TemperatureConverterActivityTests extends ActivityInstrum
entationTestCase2<TemperatureConverterActivity> {

    private TemperatureConverterActivity activity;
    private EditNumber celsiusInput;
    private EditNumber fahrenheitInput;
    private TextView celsiusLabel;
    private TextView fahrenheitLabel;
```

Then, change any cast that is present in the tests. Your IDE will highlight these; press *F2* to find them in the class.

There are still two problems we need to fix before being able to compile the test:

- We still don't have the clear() and setNumber() methods in EditNumber
- We don't have the TemperatureConverter utility class

From inside our test class, we can use the IDE to help us create the methods. Press *F2* again, and you should be taken to the error for **Cannot resolve method clear()**. Now press *Alt + Enter* to create the clear() method in type EditNumber. Same for getNumber().

Finally, we must create the TemperatureConverter class. This class will hold the mathematical conversions of Celsius and Fahrenheit, and no Android code. Therefore, we can create this package inside of our /core/ module. As previously discussed, it will be under the same package structure, only this module does not know about Android and, therefore, we can write JVM tests that run much faster.

Be sure to create it in the core module under the same package as your main code, and not in the test package.

Here's how to create that class in the core module, and the current state of our application:

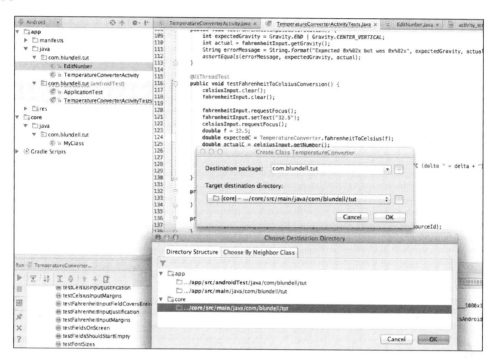

Having done this, in our test, it creates the `fahrenheitToCelsius` method.

This fixes our last problem, and leads us to a test that we can now compile and run. Yes you will have red Lint errors, but these are not "compile" errors, and so the tests can still run. (AndroidStudio's cleverness is too damn high.)

Surprisingly, or not, when we run the tests, they will fail with an exception:

```
java.lang.ClassCastException:
android.widget.EditText cannot be cast to com.blundell.tut.EditNumber
at com.blundell.tut.TemperatureConverterActivityTests.setUp(
TemperatureConverterActivityTests.java:36)
```

```
at android.test.AndroidTestRunner.runTest(
AndroidTestRunner.java:191)
```

That is because we updated all of our Java files to include our newly created `EditNumber` class, but forgot to change the layout XML.

Let's proceed to update our UI definition:

```
<com.blundell.tut.EditNumber
    android:id="@+id/converter_celsius_input"
    android:layout_width="match_parent"
    android:layout_height="wrap_content"
    android:layout_margin="@dimen/margin"
    android:gravity="end|center_vertical" />
```

That is, we replace the original `EditText` class by `com.blundell.tut.EditNumber`, which is a View extending the original `EditText` class.

Now, we run the tests again, and we discover that all tests pass.

But wait a minute; we haven't implemented any conversion or any handling of values in the new `EditNumber` class, and all tests passed with no problem. Yes, they passed because we don't have enough restrictions in our system and the ones in place, simply cancel themselves.

Before going further, let's analyze what just happened. Our test invoked the `fahrenheitInput.setText ("32.5")` method to set the temperature entered in the **Fahrenheit** field, but our `EditNumber` class doesn't do anything when text is entered, and the functionality is not implemented. So, the **Celsius** field remains empty.

The value for `expectedC` — the expected temperature in Celsius, is calculated invoking `TemperatureConverter.fahrenheitToCelsius(f)`, but this is an empty method. In this case because we knew the return type of the method we made it return to a constant 0. So, `expectedC` becomes 0.

Then, the actual value for the conversion is obtained from the UI. In this case invoking `getNumber()` from `EditNumber`. But this method was automatically generated, and to satisfy the restriction imposed by its signature, it must return a value, namely 0.

The delta value is again `0`, as calculated by `Math.abs(expectedC - actualC)`.

And finally our assertion `assertTrue(msg, delta < 0.005)` is `true`, because `delta=0` satisfies the condition, and the test passes.

So, is our methodology flawed, as it cannot detect a simple situation like this?

No, not at all, the problem here is that we don't have enough restrictions, and they are satisfied by the default values used by auto-generated methods. One alternative could be to throw exceptions at all of the auto-generated methods, something like `RuntimeException("not yet implemented")` to detect its use when not implemented. We will be adding enough restrictions in our system to easily trap this *double zero* condition.

The TemperatureConverter unit tests

It seems, from our previous experience, that the default conversion implemented always returns `0`, so we need something more robust. Otherwise, our converter will only be returning a valid result, when the parameter takes the value of 32F (32F == 0C).

The `TemperatureConverter` class is a utility class not related with the Android infrastructure, so a standard unit test will be enough to test it.

As this is the first core test we are going to write, we need to do some setup. Firstly, from the project view; in your project structure create a `test` folder under `/core/src` by selecting **New | Directory** and using the name `test`. Inside this, create a `java` folder by selecting **New | Directory,** and using the name `java`. With Gradle being magic, it will now understand that this is a place you want to add tests, and the folder should turn green (green means that the folder is a part of the test classpath). Now add a new package, technically it is not new because we are going to use `com.blundell.tut` again, by selecting **New | Package |** and using the name `com/blundell/tut`.

Now. we create our tests in our new folder and package. We create our tests by selecting **New | Java Class**, and calling it `TemperatureConverterTests`. Your project should now look like this:

Let's make our first test, inside of `TemperatureConverterTests`, press *Ctrl + Enter* to bring up the **Generate** menu, as shown in the following screenshot:

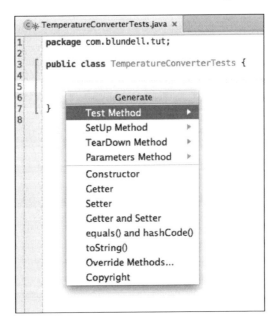

Selecting the **Test Method** test, then **JUnit4** will generate us a template method of a test that we want, name it `testFahrenheitToCelsius()`. Remember this shortcut as it's handy whenever creating a new test. Once you've generated this test, you'll notice we have compile errors on the JUnit 4 imported lines of code. Oops! we forgot to add the JUnit library to the test classpath of our core module. Open up the build file in `/core/build.gradle`, and add the JUnit dependency. Your core `build.gradle` will now look like this:

```
apply plugin: 'java''java'

dependencies {
    compile fileTree(dir: 'libs''libs', include: ['''''*.jar'])

    testCompile 'junit''junit:junit:4.+'''''
}
```

> Notice, here we have jumped from JUnit3 to JUnit4 the main difference being we can now use annotations to tell our test runner, which of the methods in the class are tests. Therefore, technically we don't need to start the methods with `test` as in `testFooBar()` anymore, but we will for our own sanity when swopping between the two (Android JUnit4 support is coming soon!).

Do a project sync by selecting **Project Sync,** and we are compiling and ready to code. Let's start writing the test:

```
@Test
public void testFahrenheitToCelsius() {
    for (double knownCelsius : conversionTable.keySet()) {
        double knownFahrenheit = conversionTable.get(knownCelsius);

        double resultCelsius =
TemperatureConverter.fahrenheitToCelsius(knownFahrenheit);

        double delta = Math.abs(resultCelsius - knownCelsius);
        String msg = knownFahrenheit + "F -> " + knownCelsius + "C"
            + "but is " + resultCelsius;
        assertTrue(msg, delta < 0.0001);
    }
}
```

Creating a conversion table with values for different temperature conversion, we know from other sources, would be a good way to drive this test:

```java
Map<Double, Double> conversionTable = new HashMap<Double, Double>() {
    // initialize (celsius, fahrenheit) pairs
    put(0.0, 32.0);
    put(100.0, 212.0);
    put(-1.0, 30.20);
    put(-100.0, -148.0);
    put(32.0, 89.60);
    put(-40.0, -40.0);
    put(-273.0, -459.40);
}};
```

To run tests in the core module, we can right click on the file in the project view, and select **Run**. As the screenshot also shows, you can use the shortcut *Cmd + Shift + F10*:

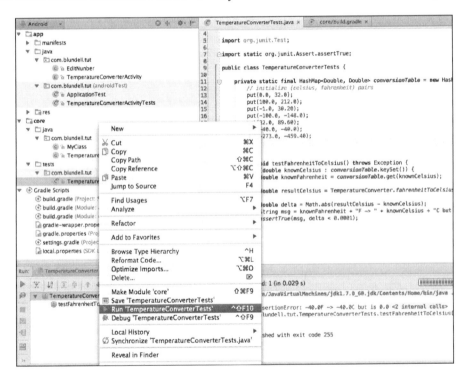

When this test runs, we verify that it fails, giving us this trace:

```
java.lang.AssertionError: -40.0F -> -40.0C but is 0.0
    at org.junit.Assert.fail(Assert.java:88)
    at org.junit.Assert.assertTrue(Assert.java:41)
    at com.blundell.tut.TemperatureConverterTests.testFahrenheitToCelsius(T
emperatureConverterTests.java:31).
```

 See how fast those core tests ran! Aim for moving as much of your application logic into your core module as you can, so you can take advantage of this speed when doing Test-driven Development.

Well, this was something we were expecting as our conversion always returns 0. Implementing our conversion, we discover that we need some ABSOLUTE_ZERO_F constant:

```java
        private static final double ABSOLUTE_ZERO_F = -459.67d;

        private static final String ERROR_MESSAGE_BELOW_ZERO_FMT =
    "Invalid temperature: %.2f%c below absolute zero";

        private TemperatureConverter() {
            // non-instantiable helper class
        }

        public static double fahrenheitToCelsius(double fahrenheit) {
            if (fahrenheit < ABSOLUTE_ZERO_F) {
                String msg = String.format(ERROR_MESSAGE_BELOW_ZERO_FMT,
    fahrenheit, 'F''F');
                throw new InvalidTemperatureException(msg);
            }
            return ((fahrenheit - 32) / 1.8d);
        }
```

Absolute zero, is the theoretical temperature at which entropy would reach its minimum value. To be able to reach this absolute zero state, according to the laws of thermodynamics, the system should be isolated from the rest of the universe. Thus, it is an unreachable state. However, by international agreement, absolute zero is defined as 0K on the Kelvin scale, and as -273.15°C on the Celsius scale or to -459.67°F on the Fahrenheit scale.

We are creating a custom exception, `InvalidTemperatureException`, to indicate a failure providing a valid temperature to the conversion method. This exception doesn't know anything about Android, and so can also sit in our core module. Create it by extending `RuntimeException`:

```
public class InvalidTemperatureException extends RuntimeException {

  public InvalidTemperatureException(String msg) {
    super(msg);
  }

}
```

Running the core tests again, we discover that `testFahrenheitToCelsius` succeeds. Therefore, we move back to our Android tests, and running these show us such that `testFahrenheitToCelsiusConversion` test fails. This tells us, that now the converter class correctly handles conversions, but there are still some problems with the UI handling this conversion.

> Don't despair about running two separate test classes. It is common for you to be selective about what tests to run; this is partly a learnt skill when doing TDD. However, if you so wish, you can write custom test runners that will run all of your tests. Also, using Gradle to run `build connectedAndroidTest` will run all your tests at once, which is advised whenever you consider you have completed a feature, or want to commit to your upstream version control.

A closer look at the `testFahrenheitToCelsiusConversion` failure trace reveals that there's something still returning `0`, when it shouldn't.

This reminds us that we are still lacking a proper `EditNumber` implementation. Before proceeding to implement the mentioned methods, let's create the corresponding tests to verify what we are implementing is correct.

The EditNumber tests

From the previous chapter, we can now determine that the best base class for our custom View tests is `AndroidTestCase`, as we need a mock `Context` class to create the custom View, but we don't need system infrastructure.

Create the tests for `EditNumber`, let's call it `EditNumberTests`, and extend `AndroidTestCase`. Reminder, this is under the app module in the `androidTest` path.

We need to add the constructors to reflect the pattern we identified before with the given name pattern:

```
public EditNumberTests() {
      this("EditNumberTests");
}

  public EditNumberTests(String name) {
      setName(name);
  }
```

The next step is to create the fixture. In this case, this is a simple `EditNumber` class that we will be testing:

```
    @Override
    protected void setUp() throws Exception {
        super.setUp();

        editNumber = new EditNumber(mContext);
        editNumber.setFocusable(true);
    }
```

The mock context is obtained from the protected field `mContext` (`http://developer.android.com/reference/android/test/AndroidTestCase.html#mContext`), available in the `AndroidTestCase` class.

At the end of the `setUp` method, we set `editNumber` as a focusable View, meaning it will be able to gain focus, as it will be participating in a bunch of tests simulating UIs that may need to request its focus explicitly.

Next, we test that the required `clear()` functionality is implemented correctly in the `testClear()` method:

```
@UiThreadTest
public void testClear() {
String value = "123.45";
        editNumber.setText(value);

        editNumber.clear();

        assertEquals("", editNumber.getText().toString());
}
```

Running the test we verify that it fails:

```
junit.framework.ComparisonFailure: expected:<[]> but was:<[123.45]>
at com.blundell.tut.EditNumberTests.testClear(EditNumberTests.java:31)
at java.lang.reflect.Method.invokeNative(Native Method)
at android.test.AndroidTestRunner.runTest(AndroidTestRunner.java:191)
```

We need to implement `EditNumber.clear()` correctly.

This is a simple case, so just by adding this implementation to `EditNumber`, we satisfy the test:

```java
public void clear() {
    setText("");
}
```

Run the test and proceed. We are going to add a new method to `EditNumber`. Here, we already have `getNumber()`, and we are adding `setNumber()` so that we can use it later on. Now let's complete the `testSetNumber()` implementation:

```java
public void testSetNumber() {

    editNumber.setNumber(123.45);

    assertEquals("123.45", editNumber.getText().toString());
}
```

Which fails unless we implement `EditNumber.setNumber()`, similar to this implementation:

```java
private static final String DEFAULT_FORMAT = "%."%.2f";";

public void setNumber(double number) {
    super.setText(String.format(DEFAULT_FORMAT, number));
}
```

We are using a constant, `DEFAULT_FORMAT`, to hold the desired format to convert the numbers. This can be later converted to a property that could also be specified in the XML layout definition of the field.

The same goes for the `testGetNumber()` and `getNumber()` pair:

```java
public void testGetNumber() {

    editNumber.setNumber(123.45);

    assertEquals(123.45, editNumber.getNumber());
}
```

And the `getNumber()` method is as follows:

```
public double getNumber() {
    String number = getText().toString();
    if (TextUtils.isEmpty(number)) {
        return 0D;
    }
    return Double.valueOf(number);
}
```

These tests succeed, so run your other tests to see where we are up to; I did this on the command line running the `gradlew build cAT` command. This runs all of the tests we have written so far; but `testFahrenheitToCelsiusConversion()` is failing. We have a lot of well tested code, take a step back, and reflect.

Here are our Android test results:

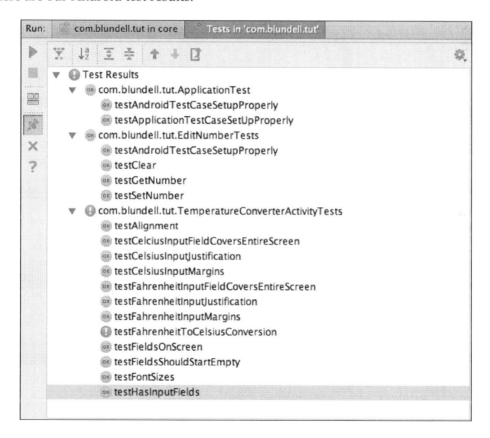

Here are our core Java test results:

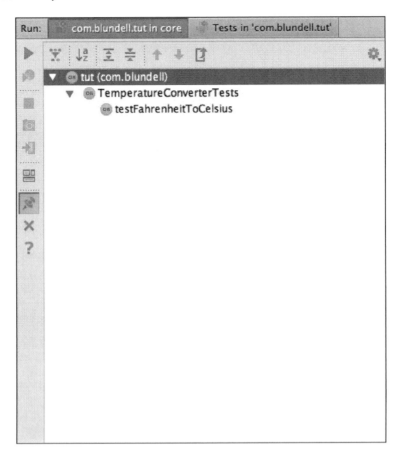

With `testFahrenheitToCelsiusConversion()` if you closely analyze the test case, can you can discover where the problem is.

Got it?

Our test method is expecting the conversion to happen automatically when the focus changes, as was specified in our list of requirements: "when one temperature is entered in one field, the other one is automatically updated with the conversion".

Remember, we don't have buttons or anything else to convert temperature values, so the conversion is to be done automatically, once the values are entered.

This leads us back to our `TemperatureConverterActivity` class, and the way it handles the conversions.

The TemperatureChangeWatcher class

One way of implementing the required behavior of constantly updating the other temperature value, is once the original has changed is through a `TextWatcher`. From the documentation, we can understand that a `TextWatcher` is an object of a type that is attached to an `Editable`; its methods will be called, when the text is changed (`http://developer.android.com/reference/android/text/TextWatcher.html`).

It seems that is what we need.

We implement this class as an inner class of `TemperatureConverterActivity`. The idea behind this is, because we act directly on the Views of the Activity, having it as an inner class shows this relationship, and keeps it obvious, should someone think of changing this Activity's layout. If you implement the minimum `TextWatcher`, your Activity will look like this:

```java
public class TemperatureConverterActivity extends Activity {

    @Override
    protected void onCreate(Bundle savedInstanceState) {
        super.onCreate(savedInstanceState);
        setContentView(R.layout.activity_temperature_converter);
    }

    /**
     * Changes fields values when the text changes; applying the
       correlated conversion method.
     */
    static class TemperatureChangedWatcher implements TextWatcher {

        @Override
        public void beforeTextChanged(CharSequence s, int start, int
          count, int after) {

        }

        @Override
        public void onTextChanged(CharSequence s, int start, int
          before, int count) {

        }

        @Override
        public void afterTextChanged(Editable s) {
```

```
          }
       }
   }
```

And now this is our code, after some additions to the recently created class:

```
/**
 * Changes fields values when the text changes;
 * applying the correlated conversion method.
 */
static class TemperatureChangedWatcher implements TextWatcher {

private final EditNumber sourceEditNumber;
private final EditNumber destinationEditNumber;
private final Option option;

private TemperatureChangedWatcher(Option option,
EditNumber source,
EditNumber destination) {
this.option = option;
   this.sourceEditNumber = source;
   this.destinationEditNumber = destination;
}

static TemperatureChangedWatcher newCelciusToFehrenheitWatcher(EditNum
ber source, EditNumber
   destination) {
return new TemperatureChangedWatcher(Option.C2F, source,
   destination);
}

static TemperatureChangedWatcher newFehrenheitToCelciusWatcher
   (EditNumber source, EditNumber destination) {
return new TemperatureChangedWatcher(Option.F2C, source,
   destination);
}

@Override
public void onTextChanged(CharSequence input, int start, int
   before, int count) {
if (!destinationEditNumber.hasWindowFocus()
|| destinationEditNumber.hasFocus()
|| input == null) {
```

```
            return;
    }

    String str = input.toString();
    if ("".equals(str)) {
        destinationEditNumber.setText("");
            return;
    }

    try {
        double temp = Double.parseDouble(str);
        double result = (option == Option.C2F)
? TemperatureConverter.celsiusToFahrenheit(temp)
: TemperatureConverter.fahrenheitToCelsius(temp);
        String resultString = String.format("%.2f", result);
        destinationEditNumber.setNumber(result);
        destinationEditNumber.setSelection(resultString.length());
        } catch (NumberFormatException ignore) {
            // WARNING this is generated whilst
    // numbers are being entered,
    // for example just a '-'
    // so we don''t want to show the error just yet
        } catch (Exception e) {
            sourceEditNumber.setError("ERROR: " +
                e.getLocalizedMessage());
        }
}


@Override
public void afterTextChanged(Editable editable) {
// not used
}


@Override
public void beforeTextChanged(CharSequence s, int start, int
    count, int after) {
// not used
}
}
```

We will be using the same `TemperatureChangeWatcher` implementation for both fields, Celsius and Fahrenheit; therefore we keep a reference to the fields used as source and destination, as well as the operation needed to update their values. To specify this operation, we are introducing `enum`, which is pure Java and so can go into the core module:

```
/**
 * C2F: celsiusToFahrenheit
 * F2C: fahrenheitToCelsius
 */
public enum Option {
    C2F, F2C
}
```

This operation is specified in the creation factory methods, and the destination and source `EditNumber` are selected accordingly. This way we can use the same watcher for different conversions.

The method of the `TextWatcher` interface we are interested in, is `onTextChanged`. This will be called any time the text changes. At the beginning, we avoid potential loops, checking who has focus, and returning if the conditions are not met.

We also set the destination field as an empty string, if the source is empty.

Finally, we try to set the resulting value of invoking the corresponding conversion method to set the destination field. We flag the error as necessary, avoiding showing premature errors, when the conversion was invoked with a partially entered number.

We need to set the listener on the input fields in `TemperatureConverterActivity.onCreate()`:

```
@Override
protected void onCreate(Bundle savedInstanceState) {
    super.onCreate(savedInstanceState);
    setContentView(R.layout.activity_temperature_converter);
    EditNumber celsiusEditNumber =
    (EditNumber) findViewById(R.id.converter_celsius_input);
    EditNumber fahrenheitEditNumber =
    (EditNumber) findViewById(R.id.converter_fahrenheit_input);
    celsiusEditNumber
    .addTextChangedListener(
```

```
newCelciusToFehrenheitWatcher(celsiusEditNumber,
   fahrenheitEditNumber));

fahrenheitEditNumber
  .addTextChangedListener(
  newFehrenheitToCelciusWatcher(fahrenheitEditNumber,
    celsiusEditNumber));
}
```

To be able to run the tests, we should compile them. To compile, we need to at least define the `celsiusToFahrenheit()` method, which is not yet defined.

More TemperatureConverter tests

We need to implement `celsiusToFahrenheit`, and as usual we start from the test.

This is fairly equivalent to the other conversion method `fahrenheitToCelsius`, and we can use the infrastructure we devised while creating this test:

```
@Test
    public void testCelsiusToFahrenheit() {
        for (double knownCelsius : conversionTable.keySet()) {
            double knownFahrenheit = conversionTable.
get(knownCelsius);

            double resultFahrenheit =
TemperatureConverter.celsiusToFahrenheit(knownCelsius);

            double delta = Math.abs(resultFahrenheit -
knownFahrenheit);
            String msg = knownCelsius + "C -> " + knownFahrenheit +
"F"
+ " but is " + resultFahrenheit;
            assertTrue(msg, delta < 0.0001);
        }
    }
```

We use the conversion table to exercise the method through different conversions, and we verify that the error is less than a predefined delta.

Then, the correspondent conversion implementation in the `TemperatureConverter` class is as follows:

```
static final double ABSOLUTE_ZERO_C = -273.15d;

public static double celsiusToFahrenheit(double celsius) {
    if (celsius < ABSOLUTE_ZERO_C) {
        String msg = String.format(
ERROR_MESSAGE_BELOW_ZERO_FMT, celsius, 'C');
        throw new InvalidTemperatureException(msg);
    }
    return (celsius * 1.8d + 32);
}
```

Now, all the tests are passing but we are still not testing all the common conditions. What I mean by this is that we have been checking the happy path so far. You should check whether errors and exceptions are correctly generated, besides all the normal cases we created so far.

Create this test to check the correct generation of exceptions, when a temperature below absolute zero is used in a conversion:

```
@Test(expected = InvalidTemperatureException.class)
public void testExceptionForLessThanAbsoluteZeroF() {
    TemperatureConverter.fahrenheitToCelsius
       (ABSOLUTE_ZERO_F - 1);
}
```

In this test, we decrement the absolute zero temperature, to obtain an even smaller value, and then we attempt the conversion. We wrote this test in our core module, and therefore used JUnit4, which allows us to use annotations to assert that we expect an exception to be thrown. If you wanted to do the same thing in JUnit3, you would have to use a try catch block, and fail the test if the code did not enter the catch block:

```
@Test(expected = InvalidTemperatureException.class)
public void testExceptionForLessThanAbsoluteZeroC() {
    TemperatureConverter.celsiusToFahrenheit(ABSOLUTE_ZERO_C - 1);
}
```

In a similar manner, we test for the exception being thrown, when the attempted conversion involves a temperature in Celsius, that is lower than the absolute zero.

The InputFilter tests

Another error requirement could be: We want to filter the input that is received by the conversion utility, so no garbage reaches this point.

The `EditNumber` class already filters valid input, and generates exceptions otherwise. We can verify this condition by creating a new test in `TemperatureConverterActivityTests`. We choose this class because we are sending keys to the entry fields, just as a real user would do:

```
public void testInputFilter() throws Throwable {
        runTestOnUiThread(new Runnable() {
            @Override
            public void run() {
                celsiusInput.requestFocus();
            }
        });
        getInstrumentation().waitForIdleSync();

        sendKeys("MINUS 1 PERIOD 2 PERIOD 3 PERIOD 4");
        double number = celsiusInput.getNumber();

        String msg = "-1.2.3.4 should be filtered to -1.234 "
            + "but is " + number;
        assertEquals(msg, -1.234d, number);
    }
```

This test requests the focus onto the Celsius field using the pattern reviewed previously. This allows us to run parts of a test in the UI thread, and send key input to the view. The keys sent are an invalid sequence containing more than one period, which is not accepted for a well-formed decimal number. It is expected that when the filter is in place, this sequence will be filtered, and only the valid characters reach the field. Asserting that the value returned by `celsiusInput.getNumber()`, is what we expect after filtering.

To implement this filter, we need to add `InputFilter` to `EditNumber`. Because this should be added to all of the constructors, we create an additional `init()` method, which we invoke from each. To achieve our goal we use an instance of `DigitsKeyListener`, accepting digits, signs, and decimal points as follows:

```
public EditNumber(Context context) {
        super(context);
        init();
    }
```

```
public EditNumber(Context context, AttributeSet attrs) {
    super(context, attrs);
    init();
}

public EditNumber(Context context, AttributeSet attrs, int
  defStyle) {
    super(context, attrs, defStyle);
    init();
}

private void init() {
  // DigistKeyListener.getInstance(true, true)
  // returns an instance that accepts digits, sign and decimal
      point
  InputFilter[] filters =
    new InputFilter[]{DigitsKeyListener.getInstance(true, true)};
    setFilters(filters);
}
```

This `init` method is invoked from each constructor, so that if this view is used programmatically or from XML, we still have our filter.

Running the tests again, we can verify that all have passed, and now everything is green again.

Viewing our final application

Well done! We now have our final application that satisfies all the requirements.

In the following screenshot we are showing one of these requirements, which is the detection of an attempt to convert a temperature below the absolute zero temperature in Celsius (-1000.00C):

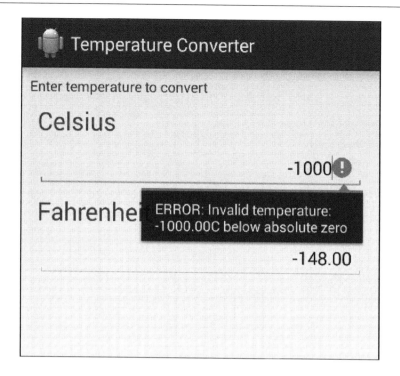

The UI respects the guidelines provided; the temperatures can be converted by entering them in the corresponding unit field.

To recap, this is the list of requirements that we have implemented:

- The application converts temperatures from Celsius to Fahrenheit, and vice versa
- The user interface presents two fields to enter the temperatures, one for Celsius and the other for Fahrenheit
- When one temperature is entered in one field, the other one is automatically updated with the conversion
- If there are errors, they should be displayed to the user, possibly using the same fields
- Some space in the user interface should be reserved for the on-screen keyboard, to ease the application operation when several conversions are entered
- Entry fields should start empty
- Values entered are decimal values with two digits after the point
- Digits are right aligned

What is more important is that we can now be certain that the application not only satisfies the requirements, but also has no evident problems or bugs. We took every step by analyzing the test results, and fixing the problems at their first appearance. This will ensure that any individual bug, once discovered, tested and fixed, will not resurface again.

Summary

We presented Test-driven Development introducing its concepts, and applying them step-by-step in a potential real-life problem.

We started with a concise list of requirements, describing the temperature converter application.

We implemented every test followed by the code that satisfies it. In this manner, we implemented the application behavior as well as its presentation, conducting tests to verify that the UI we designed follows the specifications.

Having the tests in place, lead us to analyze the different possibilities we have in running them. Evolving from the previous chapter, now our continuous integration machine can run the tests to guarantee any changes from the team will still result in a well-tested application.

The next chapter introduces Behavior-driven Development, and continues our aim for bug-free well-tested code, this time with a focus upon behavior and agreement, on what a requirement means throughout the team.

7
Behavior-driven Development

Behavior-driven Development (**BDD**) can be understood as the evolution and confluence of **Test-driven Development** (**TDD**) and acceptance testing. Both techniques were discussed in previous chapters, so you may want to look back at *Chapter 1, Getting Started with Testing,* and *Chapter 6, Practicing Test-driven Development,* before proceeding.

Behavior-driven Development introduces some new concepts, such as the use of a common vocabulary to describe the tests, and the inclusion of business participants in the software development project, such as product owners or business analysts.

We have visited Test-driven Development before, and we focused on converting low-level requirements into tests that could drive our development process. Behavior-driven Development forces us to concentrate on higher level requirements, and by using a specific vocabulary, we can express these requirements in a way that can be further analyzed or evaluated. Some people believe BDD is only the philosophy of TDD done right.

We will explore these concepts through examples, so that you can draw your own conclusions.

Given, When, and Then

Given/When/Then words are the common vocabulary that spans the divide between business and technology, and as described at `http://behaviour-driven.org`, they can also be referred to as the ubiquitous language of Behavior-driven Development. The framework is based on the following three core principles that we reproduce here, verbatim:

- Business and technology should refer to the same system in the same way
- Any system should have an identified, verifiable value to the business
- Up-front analysis, design, and planning, all have a diminishing return

Behavior-driven Development relies on the use of this specific vocabulary. Additionally, the format in which requirements are expressed is predetermined, allowing tools to interpret and execute them:

- **Given**: This is to describe the initial state before an external stimuli is received.
- **When**: This is to describe the key action the user performs.
- **Then**: This is to analyze the results of the actions. To be observable, the actions performed should have some kind of outcome.

FitNesse

FitNesse is a software development collaboration tool that can be used to manage BDD scenarios. Strictly speaking FitNesse is a set of tools, described as follows:

- As a software testing tool, FitNesse is a lightweight, open source framework that allows teams to collaborate
- It is also a Wiki where you can easily create, edit pages, and share information
- A web server, so it doesn't require additional configuration or administrative privileges to set up, or configure

Download the FitNesse distribution from `http://www.fitnesse.org`. The distribution is a JAR file that installs itself on first run. Throughout these examples, we used FitNesse standalone release 20140901 but newer versions should also work.

Running FitNesse from the command line

By default, when FitNesse runs, it listens on port 80, so to run unprivileged, you should change the port on the command line. In this example, we use `8900`:

```
$ java -jar fitnesse.jar -p 8900
```

This is the output obtained when we run the command:

```
Bootstrapping FitNesse, the fully integrated standalone wiki and
acceptance testing framework.
root page: fitnesse.wiki.fs.FileSystemPage at ./FitNesseRoot#latest
logger: none
authenticator: fitnesse.authentication.PromiscuousAuthenticator
page factory: fitnesse.html.template.PageFactory
page theme: fitnesse_straight
Starting FitNesse on port: 8900
```

Once running, you can direct your browser to the local FitNesse server home page (`http://localhost:8900/FrontPage`), and you will be presented with this content:

Creating a TemperatureConverterTests subwiki

Once FitNesse is up and running, we can start by creating a subwiki to organize our tests. You may already be familiar with the wiki concept. If not, wiki is a website that allows page editing and creation by its users. This editing process is done from within the browser, and uses a markup language that greatly simplifies the process.

 You can find out more about wikis in what could perhaps be the most famous wiki at http://en.wikipedia.org/wiki/Wiki.

Though this subwiki organization is not mandatory, it is highly recommended, especially if you plan to use FitNesse for acceptance testing on multiple projects.

One of the most simplified processes is hyperlink creation, which is done only by using *CamelCase* or *WikiWords*; that is a word that starts with a capital letter and has at least one or more capital letter in it. This WikiWord will be converted into a hyperlink to a page, with that name.

To create the **TemperatureConverterTests** subwiki, we simply press the **Edit** button to the right of the FitNesse logo, to edit the home page, adding the following:

```
| '''My Tests''' |
| TemperatureConverterTests | ''Temperature Converter Tests'' |
```

This adds a new table to the page by using the "|" markup as the first character and to delimit the columns.

We also add a column with a descriptive comment about the tests. This comment is turned into italics by surrounding it with two single quotes ("). This text will create a wiki link named, TemperatureConverterTests.

Press **Save,** and the page will be modified.

Once the page is displayed, we can verify that TemperatureConverterTests is now followed by a **[?]** (question mark) because the page has not been created yet, and will be created when we click on it. Click on it now, this puts us straight into edit mode of the new page. We can add some comments to clearly identify this newly created front page of the subwiki:

```
!contents -R2 -g -p -f -h

This is the !-TemperatureConverterTests SubWiki-!.
```

Here, the text `TemperatureConverterTests SubWiki` is escaped using `!-` and `-!` to prevent it from being converted to another page link.

Press **Save** again.

Adding child pages to the subwiki

Now, we add a new child page by using the **[Add]** link that appears next to the page title.

There are different options for creating the child page, and we can select:

- Static: This is a normal Wiki page
- Suite: This is a page containing other tests composing a suite
- Test: This is a page that contains tests

We will select to add a suite page and call it `TemperatureConverterTestSuite` as shown in the following screenshot:

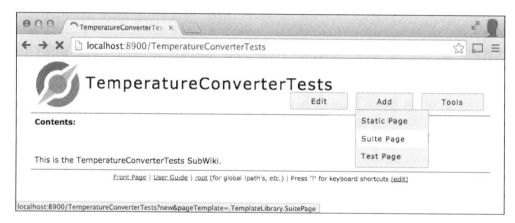

After pressing **Save**, this page is created and has been automatically added as a link to the `TemperatureConverterTests` subwiki.

Let's follow this newly created link to reach the test suite page.

Once you're here, add another child using **[Add]** | **[Test Page]**. This adds a test page, and we will name it `TemperatureConverterCelsiusToFahrenheitFixture`, as this will contain our fixture. The naming here is just a convention to organize our wiki.

Click on **Save** to finish the operation.

Adding the acceptance test fixture

Up until now, we were only creating wiki pages. Nothing exciting about that! Now, we will be adding our acceptance test fixture directly to the page. Be sure you have navigated to the newly added page, `TemperatureConverterCelsiusToFahrenheitFixture`, click on **Edit**, and replace `<test page>` with the following:

```
!contents
```

```
!|TemperatureConverterCelsiusToFahrenheitFixture       |
|celsius|fahrenheit?                                    |
|0.0    |~= 32                                          |
|100.0  |212.0                                          |
|-1.0   |30.2                                           |
|-100.0 |-148.0                                         |
|32.0   |89.6                                           |
|-40.0  |-40.0                                          |
|-273.0 |~= -459.4                                      |
|-273   |~= -459.4                                      |
|-273   |~= -459                                        |
|-273   |~= -459.40000000000003                         |
|-273   |-459.40000000000003                            |
|-273   |-459.41 <  _  < -459.40                        |
|-274.0 |Invalid temperature: -274.00C below absolute zero|
```

This table defines several items for our test feature:

- `TemperatureConverterCelsiusToFahrenheitFixture`: This is the table title and the test fixture name.
- `celsius`: This is the column name for the value we are providing as input to the test.
- `fahrenheit?`: This is the column name for the value expected as the result of the conversion. The question mark indicates that this is a result value.
- `~=`: This indicates that the result is approximately this value.
- `< _ <`: This indicates that the expected value is within this range.
- `Invalid temperature: -274.00 C below absolute zero` is the value expected by the failed conversion.

Save this content by clicking on **Save**.

Adding the supporting test classes

If we press the **Test** button, which is below the FitNesse logo (see the following screenshot for details), we will receive an error. In some way this is expected because we haven't created the supporting test fixture yet. The test fixture will be a very simple class that invokes the `TemperatureConverter` class methods.

FitNesse supports the following two different test systems:

- **fit**: This is the older of the two methods and uses HTML, parsed just prior to the fixture being called
- **slim**: This is newer; all the table processing is done inside FitNesse within slim runners

Further information about these test systems can be found at `http://fitnesse.org/FitNesse.UserGuide.WritingAcceptanceTests.TestSystems`.

In this example, we use slim, by setting the variable `TEST_SYSTEM` within the same page as follows:

```
!define TEST_SYSTEM {slim}
```

Now, we are going to create the slim test fixture. Remember the text fixture is a simple class that allows us to run our already written temperature conversion code from the FitNesse test suite. We create a new package, named `com.blundell.tut.fitnesse.fixture`, inside of our existing project `TemperatureConverter` and inside the `core` module. We will be creating the fixture inside this package.

Next, we have to create the `TemperatureConverterCelsiusToFahrenheitFixture` class, which we defined in our acceptance test table:

```java
public class TemperatureConverterCelsiusToFahrenheitFixture {
    private double celsius;
    public void setCelsius(double celsius) {
        this.celsius = celsius;
    }
    public String fahrenheit() throws Exception {
        try {
            double fahrenheit = TemperatureConverter
.celsiusToFahrenheit(celsius);
            return String.valueOf(fahrenheit);
        } catch (RuntimeException e) {
            return e.getLocalizedMessage();
        }
    }
}
```

As a reminder it should look something like this when done:

This fixture should delegate to our real code and not do anything by itself. We decided to return `String` from `fahrenheit()`, so we can return the `Exception` message in the same method.

At this point, run the core module tests to ensure you have not broken anything (and to compile the newly created class for later).

On the FitNesse test page, we should also define the package the test resides in. This allows the tests written in FitNesse to find the test fixture written in our Android project. In the same page we are still editing, add:

```
|import|
|com.blundell.tut.fitnesse.fixture|
```

Now, we add our Android project class files to the path of our FitNesse tests. This allows FitNesse to use our newly written test fixture and our `TemperatureConverter`; the code under test:

```
!path /Users/blundell/AndroidApplicationTestingGuide/core/build/classes/
test

!path /Users/blundell/AndroidApplicationTestingGuide/core/build/classes/
main
```

 This should be adapted to your system paths. The main point here is the path after `/core/`. This is pointing to where the compiled `*.class` files are for your application under test. Note, that we need to add the test sources and the project sources separately.

After finishing these steps, we can click on the **Test** button to run the tests, and the following screenshot will reflect the results:

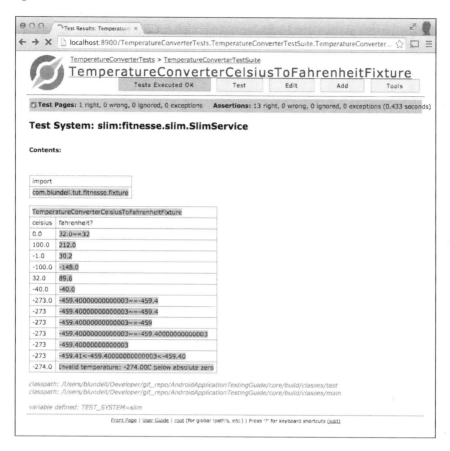

We can easily identify every test that succeeded by their green color, and the failed ones by their red color. In this example, we don't have any failure, so everything is green. Notice, it also shows the `classpath` and `TEST_SYSTEM` variables we declared.

FitNesse has another useful feature, **Test History**. All the test runs and a specific number of results are saved for a period of time, so that you can review the results later on and compare them, and thus, analyze the evolution of your changes.

This feature is accessed by clicking **Test History** located at the bottom of the list, under **Tools,** on the top menu.

In the following screenshot, we can see the results for the last 3 test runs, where 2 failed and 1 succeeded. Also by clicking on the + (plus) or - (minus) signs, you can expand or collapse the view to show or hide detailed information about the test run:

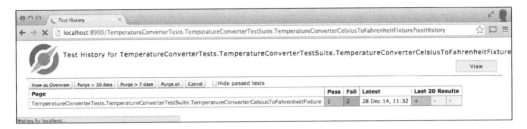

GivWenZen

GivWenZen is a framework that builds upon FitNesse and Slim to allow the user to exploit the Behavior-driven Development technique of expression, using the **Given-When-Then** vocabulary to describe tests. These test descriptions are also created using the FitNesse wiki facility, of expressing the tests as plain text contained in tables in a wiki page.

The idea is simple and straightforward, and follows up with what we have been doing with FitNesse, but this time instead of writing acceptance tests giving a table of values, we will use the three Behavior-driven Development magic words, **Given-When-Then**, to describe our scenarios.

Firstly, let's install FitNesse with GivWenZen. Download the full distribution from its download list page at `http://goo.gl/o3Hlpo`. Once unzipped, the GivWenZen JAR starts up exactly the same way as FitNesse did (because it's just a modification on top):

```
$ java -jar /lib/fitnesse.jar -p 8900
```

Further reading, comprehensive instructions and examples can be found on the wiki at `https://github.com/weswilliams/GivWenZen/wiki`. We used GivWenZen 1.0.3 in these examples, but newer versions should work as well.

The GivWenZen full distribution includes all the dependencies needed, including FitNesse, so if you have FitNesse running from previous examples it is better to stop it, as you must use a different JAR for GivWenZen.

Upon startup, point your browser to the home page and you will find a familiar FitNesse front page, or if you have configured the port like we did previously, check out some tests at `http://localhost:8900/GivWenZenTests`. You can take some time to explore the examples included.

Creating the test scenario

Let's create a simple scenario for our temperature converter, so we can understand Given-When-Then a bit better.

As a plain English sentence, our scenario would be:

Given I'm using the Temperature Converter, *When* I enter 100 into the Celsius field, *Then* I obtain 212 in the Fahrenheit field.

The value is directly translated into a GivWenZen scenario by adding this to a wiki page:

```
-|script|
|given|I'm using the !-TemperatureConverter-!|
|when |I enter 100 into the Celsius field|
|then |I obtain 212 in the Fahrenheit field|
```

The translation is straightforward. The table title must be `script`, and in this case it is preceded by a dash (-) to hide it. Then each of the **Given-When-Then** scenarios is placed in a column, and the predicate in the other column.

Before running this script, when the whole page is executed, we need to initialize GivWenZen by running another script. You do this by adding it to the top of the wiki page:

```
|import|
|org.givwenzen|
-|script|
|start|giv wen zen for slim|
```

We also need to initialize the classpath and add the corresponding imports for all scripts. Usually, this is done in one of the **SetUp** pages, which are executed before running every test script (like the `setUp()` method in a JUnit test), but for the sake of simplicity, we are adding the initialization to this same page:

```
!define TEST_SYSTEM {slim}

!path ./target/classes
!path ./target/examples
!path ./lib/clover-2.6.1.jar
!path ./lib/commons-logging.jar
!path ./lib/commons-vfs-1.0.jar
!path ./lib/dom4j-1.6.1.jar
!path ./lib/fitnesse.jar
!path ./lib/guava-18.0.jar
```

```
!path ./lib/javassist.jar
!path ./lib/log4j-1.2.9.jar
!path ./lib/slf4j-simple-1.5.6.jar
!path ./lib/slf4j-api-1.5.6.jar
!path ./givwenzen-20150106.jar
!path /Users/blundell/AndroidApplicationTestingGuide/core/build/
classes/test
!path /Users/blundell/AndroidApplicationTestingGuide/core/build/
classes/main
```

You will need to change the last two path variables to match your `TemperatureConverter` project; you'll see why you need these later.

If you run the tests at this point by clicking the **Test** button, you will receive the following message:

```
__EXCEPTION__:org.givwenzen.DomainStepNotFoundException:
```

The second column in the table, for our test outline, holds the domain steps, hence, the exception `DomainStepNotFound`. You need a step class with an annotated method matching this pattern: "I'm using the TemperatureConverter".

Typical causes of this error are as follows:

- `StepClass` is missing: This is our error
- `StepClass` is missing the `@DomainSteps` annotation
- `StepMethod` is missing the `@DomainStep` annotation
- The `StepMethod` annotation has a regular expression that does not match the current test step you have written

An example step class could be:

```
@DomainSteps
public class StepClass {
  @DomainStep("I'm using the TemperatureConverter")
  public void domainStep() {
    // TODO implement step by invoking your own code
  }
}
```

The step class should be placed in the package or subpackage of `bdd.steps`, or you could alternatively define your own custom package. This package is going to live inside the `/core/test/` module of our application. If you noticed, above the **setUp** page, we added our application on the path, so this DomainStep can be found after we build the project.

In order to use the `@DomainStep(s)` annotation in our project, we need the GivWenZen JAR on our project test path. This can be done by copying the `givwenzen.jar` file into `/core/libs`, or even better with Gradle by adding it as a remote dependency to `build.gradle`:

```
testCompile 'com.github.bernerbits:givwenzen:1.0.6.1'
```

> You'll notice that this `testCompile` dependency isn't the official GivWenZen release but someone has forked (copied) the code, and uploaded it. This doesn't matter to us for now because we are only using the two annotation classes (which I know are identical in this version), but it's worth keeping in mind and reverting to the original GivWenZen library if it is ever released as a remote dependency.

Following the small outline example, in our particular case the implementation of `StepClass` will be:

```java
package bdd.steps.tc;

import com.blundell.tut.TemperatureConverter;

import org.givwenzen.annotations.DomainStep;
import org.givwenzen.annotations.DomainSteps;

@DomainSteps
public class TemperatureConverterSteps {

    private static final String CELSIUS = "Celsius";
    private static final String FAHRENHEIT = "Fahrenheit";
    private static final String UNIT_NAME
= "(" + CELSIUS + "|" + FAHRENHEIT + ")";
    private static final String ANY_TEMPERATURE
= "([-+]?\\d+(?:\\.\\d+)?)";

    private double inputTemperature = Double.NaN;

    @DomainStep("I(?: a|')m using the TemperatureConverter")
    public void createTemperatureConverter() {
        // do nothing
    }

    @DomainStep("I enter " + ANY_TEMPERATURE
+ " into the " + UNIT_NAME + " field")
```

```
    public void setField(double inputTemperature, String unitName) {
        this.inputTemperature = inputTemperature;
    }


    @DomainStep("I obtain " + ANY_TEMPERATURE
  + " in the " + UNIT_NAME + " field")
    public boolean verifyConversion(double expectedTemperature, String
unitName) {
        double outputTemperature = convertInputInto(unitName);
        return Math.abs(outputTemperature - expectedTemperature) <
0.01D;
    }


    private double convertInputInto(String unitName) {
        double convertedInputTemperature;
        if (CELSIUS.equals(unitName)) {
            convertedInputTemperature = getCelsius();
        } else if (FAHRENHEIT.equals(unitName)) {
            convertedInputTemperature = getFahrenheit();
        } else {
            throw new RuntimeException("Unknown conversion unit" +
unitName);
        }
        return convertedInputTemperature;
    }


    private double getCelsius() {
        return TemperatureConverter.fahrenheitToCelsius(inputTemperat
ure);
    }


    private double getFahrenheit() {
        return TemperatureConverter.celsiusToFahrenheit(inputTemperat
ure);
    }
}
```

In this example, we are using a subpackage of bdd.steps because, by default, this is the package hierarchy GivWenZen searches for step's implementations. Otherwise, extra configuration is needed.

Classes implementing steps should be annotated by @DomainSteps, and each of the step's methods annotated by @DomainStep. Each step method annotation receives a String regular expression as a parameter. This regular expression is used by GivWenZen to match the steps.

For example, in our scenario, we have defined this step:

```
I enter 100 into the Celsius field
```

Our annotation is as follows:

```
@DomainStep("I enter " + ANY_TEMPERATURE
    + " into the " + UNIT_NAME + " field")
```

This will match, and the regular expression group values defined by ANY_TEMPERATURE and UNIT_NAME will be obtained and provided to the method as its argument's value and unitName:

```
public void setField(double inputTemperature, String unitName)
```

Recall that in a previous chapter I recommended reviewing regular expressions because they could be useful. Well this is probably one of these places where they are extremely useful. It allows for a flexible use of the English language. Here I(?: a|'m) was used to allow **I am** and **I'm**. In ANY_TEMPERATURE, we are matching every possible temperature value with the optional sign and decimal point. Consequently UNIT_NAME matches the unit name; that is, Celsius or Fahrenheit.

These regular expressions are used in the construction of the @DomainStep annotation parameters. Groups delimited by () parenthesis in these regular expressions are converted into method parameters. This is how setField() obtains its parameters.

Then we have a verifyConversion() method that returns true or false depending on whether the actual conversion matches the expected one, within a difference of two decimal places.

Finally, we have some methods that actually invoke the conversion methods in the TemperatureConverter class.

On running the tests once again, all the tests pass. We can confirm this by analyzing the output message:

Assertions: 1 right, 0 wrong, 0 ignored, 0 exceptions.

We should not only create scenarios for normal situations, but cover exceptional conditions as well. Say, in plain text, our scenario is something like this:

> Given I'm using the Temperature Converter, when I enter -274 into the Celsius field, then I obtain an **Invalid temperature: -274.00C below absolute zero** exception.

It can be translated into a GivWenZen table like the following:

```
-|script|
|given|I am using the !-TemperatureConverter-!                |
|when |I enter -274 into the Celsius field                     |
|then |I obtain 'Invalid temperature: -274.00C below absolute zero'
exception|
```

By adding a single supporting step method, we will be able to run it. The step method can be implemented like this:

```
    @DomainStep("I obtain '(Invalid temperature: " + ANY_TEMPERATURE +
" C|F below absolute zero)' exception")
    public boolean verifyException(String message, String value,
String unit) {
        try {
          if ( "C".equals(unit) ) {
            getFahrenheit();
          } else {
            getCelsius();
          }
        } catch (RuntimeException ex) {
          return ex.getMessage().contains(message);
        }
        return false;
    }
```

This method obtains the exception message, temperature value, and unit from the regular expression. Then this is compared against the actual exception message to verify that it matches.

Don't forget when you add Java code to your `StepClass` annotation you will need to compile the class again so that FitNesse can use the new code. One way to do this is just to run your Java tests from the IDE, forcing a recompile.

Additionally, we can create other scenarios that, in this situation, will be supported by the existing step's methods. These scenarios could be:

```
-|script|
|given |I'm using the !-TemperatureConverter-!    |
|when  |I enter -100 into the Celsius field        |
|then  |I obtain -148 in the Fahrenheit field      |

-|script|
```

```
|given |I'm using the !-TemperatureConverter-!  |
|when  |I enter -100 into the Fahrenheit field   |
|then  |I obtain -73.33 in the Celsius field      |

-|script|
|given|I'm using the !-TemperatureConverter-!                    |
|when |I enter -460 into the Fahrenheit field                    |
|then |I obtain 'Invalid temperature: -460.00F below absolute zero'
exception|
```

Because GivWenZen is based on FitNesse, we are free to combine both approaches and include the tests from our previous session, in the same suite. Doing so, we can run the entire suite from the suite page, obtaining the overall results as follows:

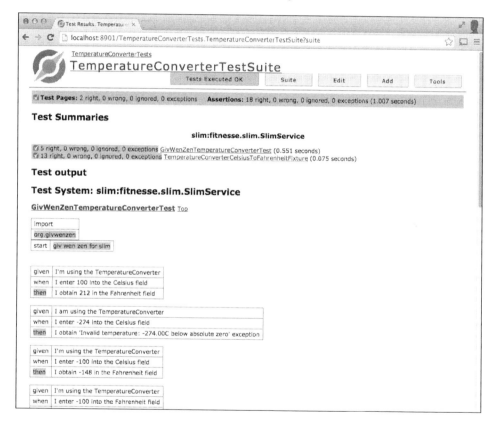

Summary

In this chapter, we discovered Behavior-driven Development as an evolution of Test-driven Development, which we examined in previous chapters.

We discussed the driving forces behind Behavior-driven Development. We analyzed the concepts serving as the foundations, explored the Given-When-Then vocabulary idea, and introduced FitNesse and Slim as helpful tools in deploying tests.

We presented GivWenZen, a tool based on FitNesse that gives us the ability to create near-English, prose-style scenarios, and test them.

We introduced these techniques and tools to our sample Android project. However, we are still limited to test subjects that are testable under the JVM, avoiding the use of Android-specific classes and the user interface. We will be exploring some alternatives to overcome this limitation in *Chapter 9, Alternative Testing Tactics*.

The next chapter deals with a different aspect of testing, concentrating on performance and profiling, which is a natural step to follow after we have our application behaving correctly, and according to our test specifications.

8
Testing and Profiling Performance

In the previous chapters, we studied and developed tests for our Android application. Those tests let us evaluate compliance against a specification and allowed us to determine whether the software was behaving correctly or not according to these rules by taking a binary verdict, whether it complied green or not. If all test cases pass, it means our software is behaving as expected. If one of the test cases fails, the software needs to be fixed.

In many other cases, mainly after we have verified that the software conforms to all these specifications, we want to move forward and know how or in what manner the criteria are satisfied. At the same time, we would want to know how the system performs under different situations to analyze other attributes such as usability, speed, response time, and reliability.

According to the Android developer guide (`http://developer.android.com/`), these are the best practices when it comes to designing our application:

- Designing for performance
- Designing for responsiveness
- Designing for seamlessness

It's extremely important to follow these best practices and to think about performance and responsiveness from the very beginning of the design. Since our application will run on Android devices with limited computer power, identifying the targets for optimization once our application is built, at least partially, and then applying the performance testing (which we will be discussing soon) can bring us bigger gains.

Donald Knuth popularized this years ago:

> "*Premature optimization is the root of all evil*".

Optimizations, which are based on guesses, intuition, and even superstition, often interfere with the design over short-term periods, and with readability and maintainability over long-term periods. On the contrary, *micro-optimizations* are based on identifying the bottlenecks or hot spots that require optimization, applying the changes, and then benchmarking again to evaluate the improvements of the optimization. So, the point we are concentrating on here is measuring the existing performance and the optimization alternatives.

This chapter will introduce a series of concepts related to benchmarking and profiling, as follows:

- Traditional logging statement methods
- Creating Android performance tests
- Using profiling tools
- Microbenchmarks using Caliper

Ye Olde Logge method

Sometimes, this is too simplistic for real-life scenarios but I'm not going to say that it could not help in some cases, mainly because its implementation takes minutes and you only need the `logcat` text output to analyze the case. This comes in handy during situations where you want to automate procedures or apply continuous integration, as described in previous chapters.

This method consists of timing a method (or a part of it), surrounding it by two time measures, and logging the difference at the end:

```
private static final boolean BENCHMARK_TEMPERATURE_CONVERSION =
    true;

@Override
public void onTextChanged(CharSequence input, int start, int
    before, int count) {
if (!destinationEditNumber.hasWindowFocus()
    || destinationEditNumber.hasFocus() || input == null) {
      return;
}

String str = input.toString();
```

```
if ("".equals(str)) {
    destinationEditNumber.setText("");
    return;
}


long t0;
if (BENCHMARK_TEMPERATURE_CONVERSION) {
    t0 = System.currentTimeMillis();
}


try {
    double temp = Double.parseDouble(str);
    double result = (option == Option.C2F)
        ? TemperatureConverter.celsiusToFahrenheit(temp)
        : TemperatureConverter.fahrenheitToCelsius(temp);
    String resultString = String.format("%.2f", result);
    destinationEditNumber.setNumber(result);
    destinationEditNumber.setSelection(resultString.length());
} catch (NumberFormatException ignore) {
    // WARNING this is generated whilst numbers are being entered,
    // for example just a '-'
    // so we don't want to show the error just yet
} catch (Exception e) {
    sourceEditNumber.setError("ERROR: " +
      e.getLocalizedMessage());
}


if (BENCHMARK_TEMPERATURE_CONVERSION) {
    long t = System.currentTimeMillis() - t0;
    Log.v(TAG, "TemperatureConversion took " + t
      + " ms to complete.");
  }
}
```

This is very straightforward. We take the times and log the difference. For this, we are using the Log.v() method, and we can see the output in the logcat when we run the application. You can control the execution of this benchmark by setting true or false to the BENCHMARK_TEMPERATURE_CONVERSION constant that you defined outside the method.

When we launch the activity with the BENCHMARK_TEMPERATURE_CONVERSION constant set to `true` in the logcat, we will receive messages like these every time the conversion takes place:

```
TemperatureConversion took 5 ms to complete.

TemperatureConversion took 1 ms to complete.

TemperatureConversion took 5 ms to complete.
```

Timing logger

Now, the one better than this is the `android.util.TimingLogger` Android class. The `TimingLogger` object can help you time your method calls without having to worry about maintaining those time variables yourself. It also has a higher degree of accuracy than `System.currentTimeMillis()`:

```java
private static final String TAG = "TemperatureTag";
@Override
public void onTextChanged(CharSequence input, int start, int before,
int count) {
if (!destinationEditNumber.hasWindowFocus()
|| destinationEditNumber.hasFocus() || input == null) {
        return;
    }

    String str = input.toString();
    if ("".equals(str)) {
      destinationEditNumber.setText("");
        return;
    }

  TimingLogger timings = new TimingLogger(TAG, "onTextChanged");
  timings.addSplit("starting conversion");

  try {
        double temp = Double.parseDouble(str);
double result = (option == Option.C2F)
    ? TemperatureConverter.celsiusToFahrenheit(temp)
    : TemperatureConverter.fahrenheitToCelsius(temp);
String resultString = String.format("%.2f", result);
        destinationEditNumber.setNumber(result);
        destinationEditNumber.setSelection(resultString.length());
} catch (NumberFormatException ignore) {
```

```
// WARNING this is generated whilst numbers are being entered,
        // for example just a '-'
// so we don't want to show the error just yet
} catch (Exception e) {
sourceEditNumber.setError("ERROR: " + e.getLocalizedMessage());
}
timings.addSplit("finish conversion");
        timings.dumpToLog();
}
```

If you launch the application now, you will notice that nothing comes out in your logcat. This is because `TimingLogger` needs you to explicitly turn on the logging for the *Tag* you defined. Otherwise, the method calls will do nothing. From a terminal, run the following command:

```
adb shell setprop log.tag.TemperatureTag VERBOSE
```

> You can check what level your logging tag is set to with the `getprop` command:
>
> `adb shell getprop log.tag.TemperatureTag`
>
> You can list all other properties from your device using this command:
>
> `adb shell getprop`

Now, when we launch the application, we will receive messages like these every time a conversion completes:

```
onTextChanged: begin
onTextChanged:        0 ms, starting conversion
onTextChanged:        2 ms, finish conversion
onTextChanged: end, 2 ms
```

Something you should take into account is that these benchmark-enabling constants should not be enabled in the production build, as other common constants, such as DEBUG or LOGD, are used. To avoid mistakes, you should integrate the verification of these constants' values in the build process you are using for automated builds, such as Gradle. Further, personally, I would remove all benchmarking or verification logging from the build before it ships to production—not comment out but delete. Remember that you can always find it again in your version control system, in the history or on a branch.

Logging code execution's speed like this is simple, but for more complex performance issues, you might want to use more detailed — though more complex — techniques.

Performance tests in Android SDK

If the previous method of adding log statements does not suit you, there are different methods of getting performance test results from our application. This is known as profiling.

When running instrumented code (as with our Android instrumented test cases), there is no standard way of getting performance test results from an Android application, as the classes used by Android tests are hidden in the Android SDK and only available to system applications, that is, applications that are built as part of the main build or system image. This strategy is not available for us, so we are not digging deeper in that direction. Instead, we will focus on other available choices.

Launching the performance test

These tests are based on an approach similar to what we just discussed, and they are used by Android to test system applications. The idea is to extend `android.app.Instrumentation` to provide performance snapshots, automatically creating a framework that we can even extend to satisfy other needs. Let's understand better what this means with a simple example.

Creating the LaunchPerformanceBase instrumentation

Our first step is to extend `Instrumentation` to provide the functionality we need. We are using a new package named `com.blundell.tut.launchperf` to keep our tests organized:

```
public class LaunchPerformanceBase extends Instrumentation {

    private static final String TAG = "LaunchPerformanceBase";

    protected Bundle results;
    protected Intent intent;

    public LaunchPerformanceBase() {
        this.results = new Bundle();
```

```
        this.intent = new Intent(Intent.ACTION_MAIN);
        this.intent.setFlags(Intent.FLAG_ACTIVITY_NEW_TASK);
        setAutomaticPerformanceSnapshots();
    }


    /**
     * Launches intent {@link #intent},
   * and waits for idle before returning.
     */
    protected void launchApp() {
        startActivitySync(intent);
        waitForIdleSync();
    }


    @Override
    public void finish(int resultCode, Bundle results) {
        Log.v(TAG, "Test results = " + results);
        super.finish(resultCode, results);
    }
}
```

We are extending `Instrumentation` here. The constructor initialized the two fields in this class: `results` and `intent`. At the end, we invoke the `setAutomaticPerformanceSnapshots()` method, which is the key here to creating this performance test.

The `launchApp()` method is in charge of starting the desired Activity and waiting before returning.

The `finish()` method logs the results received and then invokes the Instrumentation's `finish()`.

Creating the TemperatureConverterActivityLaunchPerformance class

This class sets up the Intent to invoke `TemperatureConverterActivity` and furnish the infrastructure provided by the `LaunchPerformanceBase` class to test the performance of launching our Activity:

```
public class TemperatureConverterActivityLaunchPerformance
extends LaunchPerformanceBase {

    @Override
```

```
    public void onCreate(Bundle arguments) {
        super.onCreate(arguments);
        String className = "com.blundell.tut.
TemperatureConverterActivity";
        intent.setClassName(BuildConfig.APPLICATION_ID, className);
        start();
    }

    @Override
    public void onStart() {
        super.onStart();
        launchApp();
        finish(Activity.RESULT_OK, results);
    }
}
```

Here, `onCreate()` calls `super.onCreate()` as the Android lifecycle dictates.
Then the Intent is set, specifying the class name and the package. Then one of the
Instrumentation's methods, `start()`, is called. It creates and starts a new thread in
which to run instrumentation. This new thread will make a call to `onStart()`, where
you can implement the instrumentation.

Then the `onStart()` implementation follows, invoking `launchApp()` and `finish()`.

Running the tests

To be able to run this test, we need to define the specific Instrumentation in the
`Build.gradle` file of the `TemperatureConverter` project.

This is the snippet of code we have to add to the `app/build.gradle`:

```
defaultConfig {
        // other code

        testInstrumentationRunner "com.blundell.tut.launchperf.
TemperatureConverterActivityLaunchPerformance"
    }
```

Once everything is in place, we are ready to start running the test.

First, install the APK that includes these changes. Then, we have several options to run the tests, as we reviewed in previous chapters. In this case, we are using the command line, as it is the easiest way of getting all the details. If you only have one device connected, use this:

```
$ adb shell am instrument -w com.blundell.tut.test/com.blundell.tut.
launchperf.TermeratureConverterActivityLaunchPerformance
```

 If you are ever wondering what `Instrumentation` test runners you have installed on your device, you can use this command:

```
adb shell pm list instrumentation
```

We receive the set of results for this test in the standard output:

```
IINSTRUMENTATION_RESULT: other_pss=7866
INSTRUMENTATION_RESULT: global_alloc_count=4009
INSTRUMENTATION_RESULT: java_allocated=7271
INSTRUMENTATION_RESULT: execution_time=347
INSTRUMENTATION_RESULT: gc_invocation_count=0
INSTRUMENTATION_RESULT: native_pss=0
INSTRUMENTATION_RESULT: received_transactions=-1
INSTRUMENTATION_RESULT: other_shared_dirty=7128
INSTRUMENTATION_RESULT: native_shared_dirty=0
INSTRUMENTATION_RESULT: java_free=4845
INSTRUMENTATION_RESULT: java_size=12116
INSTRUMENTATION_RESULT: global_freed_size=155012
INSTRUMENTATION_RESULT: java_pss=1095
INSTRUMENTATION_RESULT: pre_sent_transactions=-1
INSTRUMENTATION_RESULT: java_private_dirty=884
INSTRUMENTATION_RESULT: pre_received_transactions=-1
INSTRUMENTATION_RESULT: other_private_dirty=6228
INSTRUMENTATION_RESULT: native_private_dirty=0
INSTRUMENTATION_RESULT: cpu_time=120
INSTRUMENTATION_RESULT: sent_transactions=-1
INSTRUMENTATION_RESULT: native_allocated=10430
INSTRUMENTATION_RESULT: java_shared_dirty=8360
INSTRUMENTATION_RESULT: global_freed_count=1949
INSTRUMENTATION_RESULT: native_free=14145
INSTRUMENTATION_RESULT: native_size=10430
INSTRUMENTATION_RESULT: global_alloc_size=372992
INSTRUMENTATION_CODE: -1
```

We have highlighted two of the values we are interested in: `execution_time` and `cpu_time`. They account for the total execution time and the CPU time used respectively.

Running this test on an emulator increases the potential for mismeasurement, because the host computer is running other processes, which also take up the CPU, and the emulator does not necessarily represent the performance of a real piece of hardware.

Needless to say, in this and any other case where you measure something that is variable over time, you should use a measurement strategy and run the test several times to obtain different statistical values, such as average or standard deviation.

Using the Traceview and dmtracedump platform tools

The Android SDK includes among its various tools two that are specially intended to analyze performance problems and profiles, and potentially determine the target to apply optimizations. Android also offers us the **Dalvik Debug Monitor Service** (**DDMS**), which collates these tools all in one place. DDMS can be opened from Android Studio by navigating to **Tools | Android | Device Monitor**, or from the command line with the command monitor. You can use Traceview and other tools inside DDMS by using handy GUI shortcuts. Here, however, we are going to use the command-line options so that you can understand the tools behind the GUI.

These tools have an advantage over other alternatives: usually, no modification to the source code is needed for simpler tasks. However, for more complex cases, some additions are needed, but they are very simple, as we will see shortly.

If you don't need precision about starting and stopping tracing, you can drive it from the command line or Android Studio. For example, to start tracing from the command line, you can use the following command. Remember to add the serial number with `-s` if you have multiple devices attached:

```
$ adb shell am start -n com.blundell.tut/.TemperatureConverterActivity
$ adb shell am profile com.blundell.tut start /mnt/sdcard/tc.trace
```

Do something such as entering a temperature value in the Celsius field to force a conversion, then run this:

```
$ adb shell am profile com.blundell.tut stop
$ adb pull /mnt/sdcard/tc.trace /tmp/tc.trace
```

```
7681 KB/s (1051585 bytes in 0.133s)
```

```
$ traceview /tmp/tc.trace
```

Otherwise, if you need more precision about when profiling starts, you can add the programmatic style:

```
@Override
public void onTextChanged(CharSequence input, int start, int
  before, int count) {
  if (!destinationEditNumber.hasWindowFocus()
          || destinationEditNumber.hasFocus() || input == null) {
    return;
  }
String str = input.toString();
if ("".equals(str)) {
  destinationEditNumber.setText("");
  return;
}


if (BENCHMARK_TEMPERATURE_CONVERSION) {
Debug.startMethodTracing();
}

try {
double temp = Double.parseDouble(str);
  double result = (option == Option.C2F)
      ? TemperatureConverter.celsiusToFahrenheit(temp)
      : TemperatureConverter.fahrenheitToCelsius(temp);
String resultString = String.format("%.2f", result);
  destinationEditNumber.setNumber(result);
  destinationEditNumber.setSelection(resultString.length());
} catch (NumberFormatException ignore) {
// WARNING this is generated whilst numbers are being entered,
  // for example just a '-'
// so we don't want to show the error just yet
} catch (Exception e) {
  sourceEditNumber.setError("ERROR: " + e.getLocalizedMessage());
}

  if (BENCHMARK_TEMPERATURE_CONVERSION) {
    Debug.stopMethodTracing();
  }
}
```

This will create a trace file, using the default name, `dmtrace.trace`, on the SD card by invoking `Debug.startMethodTracing()`, which starts method tracing with the default log name and buffer size. When we are done, we call `Debug.stopMethodTracing()` to stop the profiling.

> Remember that enabling profiling really slows down the application execution, so the results should be interpreted by their relative weight, not by their absolute values.
>
> To be able to write to the SD card, the application requires an `android.permission.WRITE_EXTERNAL_STORAGE` permission to be added to the manifest.
>
> For Traceview using DDMS, the stream is sent through the JDWP connection straight to your development computer, and the permission is not needed.

You need to exercise the application in order to obtain the trace file. This file needs to be pulled to the development computer to be further analyzed using `traceview`:

```
$ adb pull /mnt/sdcard/dmtrace.trace /tmp/dmtrace.trace
   8491 KB/s (120154 bytes in 0.013s)
$ traceview /tmp/dmtrace.trace
```

After running this command, the traceview's window appears, displaying all the information collected, as shown in this screenshot:

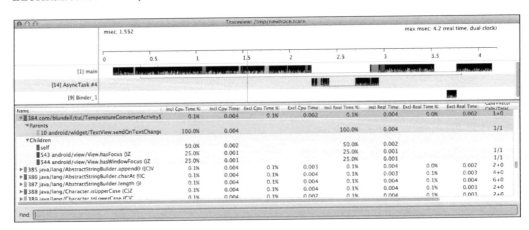

The top part of the window shows the timeline panel and a colored area for every method. Time increases to the right along the scale. There are also small lines under the colored row, displaying the extent of all the calls to the selected method.

We profiled a small segment of our application, so only the main thread was running from our process. In the cases where other threads run during the profiling, this information will also be displayed. For instance, this shows that an AsyncTask was executed by the system.

The bottom part shows the profile panel, every method executed, and its parent-child relationships. We refer to calling methods as **parents** and the called methods as **children**. When clicked on, a method expands to show its parents and children. Parents are shown with a purple background and children with a yellow background.

Also, the color selected for the method, done in a round-robin fashion, is displayed before the method name.

Finally, at the bottom, there's a **Find:** field, where we can enter a filter to reduce the amount of information displayed. For example, if we are interested in displaying only the methods in the `com.blundell.tut` package, we should enter `com/blundell/tut`.

Clicking on a column will set the order of the list according to that column in ascending or descending order.

This table shows you the available columns and their descriptions:

Column	Description
Name	The name of the method, including its package name, in the form we just described, which is by using / (slash) as the delimiter. Also, the parameters and the return type are displayed.
Incl Cpu Time%	The inclusive time, as a percentage of the total time, used by the method. This includes all its children.
Incl Cpu Time	The inclusive time, in milliseconds, used by the particular method. This includes the method and all its children.
Excl Cpu Time%	The exclusive time, as a percentage of the total time, used by the method. This excludes all its children.
Excl Cpu Time	The exclusive time, in milliseconds. This is the total time spent in the particular method. It excludes all its children.
Incl Real Time%	Inclusive time plus the waiting time of the process to execute as a percentage (waiting for I/O).
Incl Real Time	Inclusive time plus the waiting time of the process to execute.
Excl Real Time%	Exclusive time plus the waiting time of the process to execute as a percentage (waiting for I/O).
Excl Real Time	Exclusive time plus the waiting time of the process to execute.

Column	Description
Calls+Recur Calls/Total	This column shows the number of calls for the particular method and the number of recursive calls. The number of calls compared with the total number of calls made to this method.
Cpu Time/ Call	The time of every call in milliseconds.

The final word on Traceview is a word of warning: Traceview currently disables the JIT compiler from running, which may cause Traceview to misattribute time to code blocks, which the JIT may be able to win back. Therefore, it is imperative after making changes you imply from Traceview data, that you ensure that the resulting code actually runs faster when run without Traceview.

Dmtracedump

Dmtracedump is an alternative to traceview. It allows you to generate your trace data in alternative formats, including HTML, and also a call-stack diagram, using the trace files already gathered. The later diagram is of a tree structure, and each node of the tree represents one call in the stack.

You can use the same traceview files we have pulled from the device with the new command:

```
dmtracedump -t 40 -g dmtrace.png /tmp/dmtrace.trace
```

When running dmtracedump, if you get the **dot command not found** error and no `*.png` file output, it means you need to install GraphViz. GraphViz creates the visual graphical output of your trace. You can read more about it and download it at www.graphviz.org. Once it is installed, your error should go away.

The graphs produced can be very big, and it's recommended that you pass a detailed but pinpointing trace file so that your output is directed towards your code as much as possible, Alternatively, as we just did, you can make use of the -t parameter so that you attempt to include only those child nodes that take up a fair amount of CPU time (such as your foreground app code). Here is a snippet of the graph produced from a trace when we enter a temperature conversion:

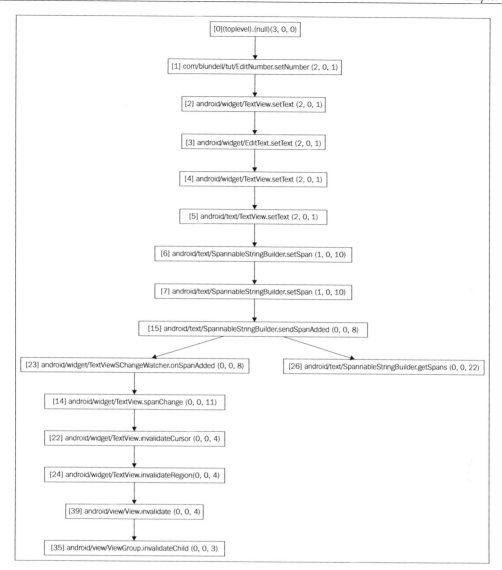

To view your trace data as HTML, run the following:

```
dmtracedump -h /tmp/dmtrace.trace > dmtrace.html
```

This alternative HTML view allows you to navigate around the details of your trace and filter the call stacks of each call, in a way different from how the original traceview GUI does:

Table of Contents

- Exclusive profile
- Inclusive profile
- Class/method profile
- Method/class profile

[Top] [Exclusive] [Inclusive] [Class] [Method]

Total cycles: 3526

Exclusive elapsed times for each method, not including time spent in children, sorted by exclusive time.

```
Usecs  self %  sum %  Method
  156    4.42   4.42  [26] android/text/SpannableStringBuilder.getSpans (IILjava/lang/Class;)[Ljava/lang/Object;
   83    2.35   6.78  [64] java/lang/Class.isInstance (Ljava/lang/Object;)Z
   50    1.42   8.20  [100] android/text/PackedIntVector.size ()I
   49    1.39   9.59  [104] android/graphics/Paint.native_getTextRunAdvances (I[CIIIII[FI)F
   46    1.30  10.89  [7] android/text/SpannableStringBuilder.setSpan (ZLjava/lang/Object;III)V
   45    1.28  12.17  [14] android/widget/TextView.spanChange (Landroid/text/Spanned;Ljava/lang/Object;IIII)V
   44    1.25  13.41  [73] android/text/DynamicLayout.getLineCount ()I
   44    1.25  14.66  [79] android/text/PackedIntVector.getValue (II)I
   43    1.22  15.88  [35] android/view/ViewGroup.invalidateChild (Landroid/view/View;Landroid/graphics/Rect;)V
   42    1.19  17.07  [118] java/util/concurrent/ThreadPoolExecutor$Worker.tryAcquire (I)Z
```

This table describes the extra command-line arguments you can use with dmtracedump:

Command	Description
-d <trace-file-name>	Carry out a comparison against this trace file and print the difference.
-g <graph-out-file-name.png>	Generate the graph in this file. Technically, it might not generate PNG images, but if you name it something.png, you can open the file to see the graph.
-h	Turn on the HTML output. This will be printed on your console just as HTML code, so remember to pipe this output to a file, such as example.html.
-o	Dump the trace file instead of profiling.
-s <trace-file-name>	URL base to the location of the sortable JavaScript file (I'm not sure what the use of this parameter is! https://code.google.com/p/android/issues/detail?id=53468).
-t <percent>	Minimum threshold for including child nodes in the graph (the child's inclusive time as a percentage of the parent's inclusive time). If this option is not used, the default threshold is 20 percent.

Microbenchmarks

Benchmarking is the act of running a computer program or operation in order to compare operations in a way that produces quantitative results, normally by running a set of tests and trials against them.

Benchmarks can be organized in the following two big categories:

- Macrobenchmarks
- Microbenchmarks

Macrobenchmarks exist as a means to compare different platforms in specific areas such as processor speed, number of floating-point operations per unit of time, graphics and 3D performance, and so on. They are normally used against hardware components, but can also be used to test software-specific areas, such as compiler optimization or algorithms.

As opposed to these traditional macrobenchmarks, a **microbenchmark** attempts to measure the performance of a very small piece of code, often a single method. The results obtained are used to choose between competing implementations that provide the same functionality, when deciding the optimization path.

The risk here is to microbenchmark something different than what you think you are measuring. This is something to take into account mainly in the case of JIT compilers, as used by Android, starting with version 2.2 Froyo. The JIT compiler may compile and optimize your microbenchmark differently than the same code in your application. So, be cautious when taking your decision.

This is different from the profiling tactic introduced in the previous section, as this approach does not consider the entire application but a single method or algorithm at a time.

Caliper microbenchmarks

Caliper is Google's open source framework for writing, running, and viewing results of microbenchmarks. There are many examples and tutorials on its website at `http://code.google.com/p/caliper`.

Caliper is endorsed on `developer.android.com` and is used by Google to measure the performance of the Android programming language itself. We are exploring its essential use here, and will introduce more Android-related usage in the next chapter.

Its central idea is to benchmark methods, mainly to understand how efficient they are. We may decide that this is the target for our optimization, perhaps after analyzing the results provided by profiling the app via Traceview.

Caliper benchmarks use annotations to help you build your tests correctly. Benchmarks are structured in a fashion similar to JUnit tests. Previously, Caliper mirrored JUnit3 in its conventions; for instance, where tests had to start with the prefix `test`, benchmarks started with the prefix `time`. With the latest version, it is like JUnit4 where JUnit has `@Test`, Caliper uses `@Benchmark`. Every benchmark then accepts an int parameter, usually named `reps`, indicating the number of repetitions to benchmark the code that sits inside the method, which is surrounded by a loop counting the repetitions.

The `setUp()` method or `@Before` annotation is present and is used as `@BeforeExperiment`.

Benchmarking the temperature converter

Let's start by creating a new Java module inside our project. Yes, this time, it is not an Android module—just Java.

For consistency, use the `com.blundell.tut` package as the main package.

Add a dependency to this module on your core module in the `/benchmark/build.gradle` file. This allows you to access the temperature converter code:

```
compile project(':core').
```

Also, add the `Caliper` library as a dependency; this is hosted on Maven central. However, at the time of writing this book, the version released by Google is Caliper 1.0-beta-1, which does not include the annotations we have just discussed. I have tried to poke them to fix this, at `https://code.google.com/p/caliper/issues/detail?id=291`, star that issue if you feel so inclined. Therefore, in the meantime, another developer has released Caliper under his package to Maven central to allow us to use annotations. This is the import you need:

```
compile 'net.trajano.caliper:caliper:1.1.1'
```

Create the `TemperatureConverterBenchmark` class that will be containing our benchmarks:

```
public class TemperatureConverterBenchmark {

  public static void main(String[] args) {
CaliperMain.main(CelsiusToFahrenheitBenchmark.class, args);
  }

  public static class CelsiusToFahrenheitBenchmark {

   private static final double MULTIPLIER = 10;
```

```
@Param({"1", "10", "100"})
int total;

private List<Double> temperatures = new ArrayList<Double>();

@BeforeExperiment
public void setUp() {
    temperatures.clear();
    generateRandomTemperatures(total);
}

private void generateRandomTemperatures(int total) {
    Random r = new Random(System.currentTimeMillis());
    for (int i = 0; i < total; i++) {
        double randomTemperature = MULTIPLIER * r.nextGaussian();
        temperatures.add(randomTemperature);
    }
}

@Benchmark
public void timeCelsiusToFahrenheit(int reps) {
for (int i = 0; i < reps; i++) {
    for (double t : temperatures) {
        TemperatureConverter.celsiusToFahrenheit(t);
    }
}
    }
    }
}
```

We have a setUp() method similar to JUnit tests that use the @BeforeExperiment annotation. It is run before the benchmarks are run. This method initializes a collection of random temperatures used in the conversion benchmark. The size of this collection is a field and is annotated here with the @Param annotation so that Caliper knows about its existence. Caliper will allow us to provide the value of this parameter when we run the benchmarks. However, for this example, we have given the param some default values of "1", "10", "100". This means we will have at least three benchmarks, with one, then 10, and then 100 values of temperature.

We use a Gaussian distribution for the pseudo-random temperatures, as this can be a good model of the reality of a user.

The benchmark method itself uses the `@Benchmark` annotation so that caliper can recognize and run this method, in this `timeCelsiusToFahrenheit()` instance. Inside this method, we loop for the number of repetitions passed to us as a method parameter, each time invoking the `TemperatureConverter.celsiusToFahrenheit()` conversion, which is the method we wish to benchmark.

Running Caliper

To run Caliper, right-click on the class and select from the menu and run `TemperatureConverterBenchmark.main()`. If you want to change the total parameter from the default of `1, 10, 100`, edit the run configuration, and in the Program arguments field, input `-Dtotal=5,50,500`.

Either way, this will run the benchmarks, and if everything goes well, we will be presented with the results:

```
Experiment selection:
  Instruments:      [allocation, runtime]
  User parameters:  {total=[1, 10, 100]}
  Virtual machines: [default]
  Selection type:   Full cartesian product


This selection yields 6 experiments.
Starting trial 1 of 6: {instrument=allocation, benchmarkMethod=timeCelsiu
sToFahrenheit, vm=default, parameters={total=1}}… Complete!
  bytes(B): min=32.00, 1st qu.=32.00, median=32.00, mean=32.00, 3rd
qu.=32.00, max=32.00
  objects: min=1.00, 1st qu.=1.00, median=1.00, mean=1.00, 3rd qu.=1.00,
max=1.00

….

Starting trial 6 of 6: {instrument=runtime, benchmarkMethod=timeCelsiusTo
Fahrenheit, vm=default, parameters={total=100}}… Complete!
  runtime(ns): min=158.09, 1st qu.=159.52, median=161.16, mean=162.42,
3rd qu.=163.06, max=175.13
Execution complete: 1.420m.
Collected 81 measurements from:
  2 instrument(s)
  2 virtual machine(s)
  3 benchmark(s)

Results have been uploaded. View them at: https://microbenchmarks.
appspot.com/runs/33dcd3fc-fde7-4a37-87d9-aa595b6c9224
```

To help visualize these results, there is a service hosted on Google AppEngine (http://microbenchmarks.appspot.com) that accepts your result data and lets you visualize it in a much better way. You can see this URL in the preceding output, where the results have been published.

If you wish to access a suite of benchmarks, or collate your results over time, you can log in to this server and gain an API key to help congregate your results. Once you have obtained this key, it should be placed in the `~/.caliper/config.properties` file in your home directory, and the next time you run the benchmarks, the results will be linked to your login.

The `config.properties` will look like this snippet after you pasted the API key obtained:

```
# Caliper config file
# Run with --print-config to see all of the options being applied
# INSTRUMENT CONFIG
# instrument.micro.options.warmup=10s
# instrument.micro.options.timingInterval=500ms
# instrument.micro.options.reportedIntervals=7
# instrument.micro.options.maxRuntime=10s
# VM CONFIG
vm.args=-Xmx3g -Xms3g
# See the Caliper webapp to get a key so you can associate results
with your account
results.upload.options.key=abc123-a123-123a-b123-a12312312
```

The result will be as follows:

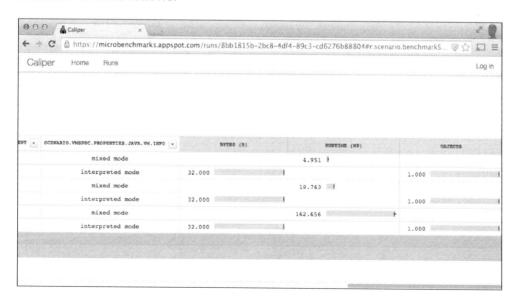

As well as the run speeds, the generated website shows you the configuration of the JVM used to run the tests. The blue and red sections are expandable for seeing more properties, helping you to detect when the environment being run on is actually affecting the different results being reported.

Summary

In this chapter, we dissected the available alternatives for testing the performance measures of our application by benchmarking and profiling our code.

Some options that should be provided by the Android SDK are not available at the time of writing this book, and there is no way to implement Android PerformanceTestCases because some of the code is hidden in the SDK. We visited and analyzed some other valid alternatives.

Among these alternatives, we found that we can use simple log statements or more sophisticated code that extends instrumentation.

Subsequently, we analyzed profiling alternatives and described and exemplified the use of traceview and dmtracedump.

Finally, you discovered Caliper, a microbenchmarking tool that has native support for Android. However, we introduced its most basic usage, and postponed more specific Android and Dalvik VM usage for the next chapter.

To be able to quantify your testing efforts in the next chapter, we will be executing coverage reports on our code. We will also introduce alternative testing and discuss new upcoming libraries and topics in the Android testing world to hopefully give you some jumping-off points to explore and continue on your own testing voyage.

9
Alternative Testing Tactics

Up to this point, we have analyzed the most common and accessible tactics to implement testing in our projects. However, there are a few missing pieces in our puzzle, which we'll hope to cover in this final chapter. The Android ecosystem is always moving forward, with the advent of Android Studio and Gradle. The toolbox for testing is also always being added too. In this area, we'll look at some third-party libraries that can help us expand our testing framework; such as Robolectric for Android testing on the JVM, as well as potential bleeding edge and future developments, like Fork; imagine threading for your tests.

In this chapter, we will be covering the following topics:

- Jacoco code coverage
- Robotium
- Testing on host's JVM
- Robolectric
- Fest
- Spoon/Fork

Code coverage

Perhaps Android's Achilles' heel would be the lack of documentation, and the number of places you have to visit to get the complete version of what you are trying to find, or what's even worse, in many cases the official documentation is incorrect, or has not been updated to match the current release. The documentation for the new Gradle build system is very sparse on the ground, and this is where most people start when trying to read up on code coverage; so let's light up a few dark corners.

Code coverage is a measure used in software testing that describes the amount of source code that was actually tested by the test suite, and to what degree, following some criteria. As code coverage inspects the code directly, it is therefore a form of white box testing.

> White-box testing (also known as clear box testing, glass box testing, transparent box testing, and structural testing), is a method of testing software that tests internal structures or workings of an application, as opposed to its functionality (say black-box testing).

From the several tools available, providing code coverage analysis for Java we are using Jacoco, an open-source toolkit for measuring and reporting Java code coverage that is supported by the Android project. The infrastructure to start using it for your own projects is already there, therefore, minimizing the effort needed to implement it. Jacoco supersedes the EMMA code coverage tool, while taking knowledge from lessons learned in this endeavor, and being built by the same team.

Jacoco distinguishes itself from other tools by going after a distinctive feature combination; support for large-scale enterprise software development, while keeping individual developer's work fast and iterative. This is fundamental in a project the size of Android, and Jacoco shines at its best, providing code coverage for it.

Jacoco features

Java, the Android Gradle plugin and the Gradle build system, all have native support for Jacoco. From the latest Jacoco version available at this book's release, paraphrasing its documentation, the most distinctive set of features are the following:

- Jacoco can instrument classes for coverage either offline (before they are loaded) or on the fly (using an instrumenting application classloader).

- Supported coverage types: class, method, line, branch, and instruction. Jacoco can detect when a single source code line is covered only partially.

- Coverage stats are aggregated at method, class, package, and "all classes" levels.

- Output report types: plain text, HTML, XML. All report types support drill-down to a user-controlled detail depth. The HTML report supports source code linking.

- Output reports can highlight items with coverage levels, below user-provided thresholds.

- Coverage data obtained in different instrumentation or test runs can be merged together.

- Jacoco does not require access to the source code and degrades gracefully with decreasing amounts of debug information available in the input classes.

- Jacoco is relatively fast; the runtime overhead of added instrumentation is small (5 to 20%), and the bytecode instrumentor itself is very fast (mostly limited by file I/O speed). Memory overhead is a few hundred bytes per Java class.

Temperature converter code coverage

The Android Gradle plugin has support for Jacoco code coverage out of the box. The setup involves selecting which build flavor you want to obtain coverage reports for, and selecting your Jacoco version. We want to instrument our debug flavor so that we can have coverage without affecting release code. Under the android closure, add these lines to your android/build.gradle file:

```
android {
    ...
    buildTypes {
        debug {
            testCoverageEnabled true
        }
    }

    jacoco {
        version = '0.7.2.201409121644'
    }
}
```

The Jacoco version does not actually have to be added here, however, the version of Jacoco shipping with Android is currently behind the latest release. The latest version of the Jacoco coverage library can be found on their GitHub page at https://github.com/jacoco/jacoco or Maven central. Therefore, it is recommended that you make the version explicit.

Generating code coverage analysis report

You will need to have an emulator running as Jacoco instruments your android tests, and these are run on a device so an emulator is appropriate. When the tests are complete, a code coverage report is generated on the device and then pulled to your local machine. If you choose to use a real device instead of an emulator, it will need to be rooted. Otherwise this pull of the reports will fail with a `Permission Denied` exception.

Run code coverage from the command line as follows:

```
$./gradlew build createDebugCoverageReport
```

Alternatively, you can use this command if you have multiple flavors:

```
$./gradlew build connectedCheck
```

This following message verifies that our tests have been run and the coverage data is retrieved:

`:app:connectedAndroidTest`

`:app:createDebugCoverageReport`

`:app:connectedCheck`

`BUILD SUCCESSFUL`

This has created the report files inside the `/app/build/outputs/reports/coverage/debug/` directory. If you use multiple flavors, your path will be slightly different.

Now before we go any further, if you haven't realized yet, we have not only been generating the report for the Android app module, but we also have code in our Java `core` module. Let's create a report for this as well.

With Gradle having support for Jacoco, we only need to apply the Jacoco plugin to our `code/build.gradle` file:

```
apply plugin: 'jacoco''jacoco''jacoco''jacoco'''
```

More configurations are possible with the same closure that we are using for our Android module. Details of properties that can be changed are found on the Gradle Jacoco plugin website at `http://gradle.org/docs/current/userguide/jacoco_plugin.html`.

Now, if you run the `./gradlew` command tasks, you should see a new Gradle task that is generated, `jacocoTestReport`. Run this task to generate code coverage for our core module:

```
$./gradlew jacocoTestReport
```

This has created the report files inside the `/core/build/reports/jacoco/test/` directory.

Excellent! Now we have code coverage reports for both our `app` code and our `core` code.

> It is possible to take both of these reports and merge them into one file. You will most likely have to work with the XML output to do this. This is left as a task for the reader but take a look on the Jacoco website and the Gradle plugin site for hints (it has been done before).

Let's open the `app` modules `index.html` to display the coverage analysis report.

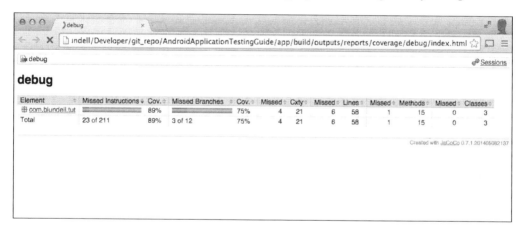

The information presented in the report includes coverage metrics in a way that allows drilling down into data, in a top-down fashion, starting with all classes, and going all the way to the level of individual methods and source lines (in the HTML report).

The fundamental component of code coverage in Jacoco is the basic block; all other types of coverage are derived from the basic block coverage in some way. Line coverage is mostly used to link to the source code.

This table describes the important pieces of information in the Jacoco coverage report:

Label	Description
Element	The name of the class or package.
Missed Instructions, Coverage	A visual indicator showing the number of instructions not covered by tests (in red), next to the percentage of instructions covered by tests. Example: if (x = 1 && y = 2) would be two instructions but one line of code.
Missed Branches, Coverage	A visual indicator of the number of branches not covered by tests (in red), next to the percentage of branches covered. Think of an if/else statement as two branches. The number of branches in a method is a good measure of its complexity.
Missed, Cxty	The number of complex paths (cyclomatic complexity) missed, next to the total complexity. A complexity path is defined as a sequence of bytecode instructions, without any jumps or jump targets. Adding a branch to the code (an if statement) would add two pathways (true or false), thus making the complexity increase by 1. However, adding an instruction (x = 1;) would not increase the complexity.
Missed, Lines	The number of lines not executed by any test, next to the total number of lines.
Missed, Methods	The number of methods missed, next to the total number of methods. This is a basic Java method that is composed by a given number of basic paths.
Missed, Classes	The number of classes without a single test, next to the total number of classes.

We can drill-down from the package to classes, to specific methods, and the lines covered are presented in green, uncovered ones appear in red, while partially covered ones are in yellow.

This is an example of the report for the **core/**TemperatureConverter class:

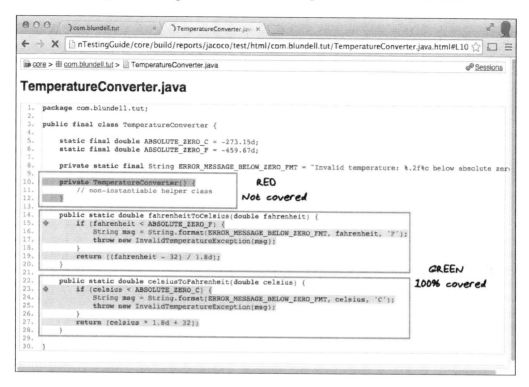

In this report, we can see that the class TemperatureConverter is not 100% covered. When we look into the code, it is the constructor that is never tested.

Do you know why? Think for a moment.

Yes, because a private constructor is never called. This is a utility class that is not supposed to be instantiated at all.

If you can imagine creating a new class with just a static method, you don't often create the private constructor; it would be left as the non-visible default public constructor. In this case, I have been rather diligent and wrote this private constructor, because I was a good boy scout at the time (and still am!).

We can see here not only how this analysis is helping us to test our code and find potential bugs, but also to improve the design.

Once we consider this private constructor as a sensible piece of code not to be running tests upon, we can see now that even though the class is not yet 100 percent covered and thus not green, we can be assured that this constructor won't be invoked from any other class.

I think a very important lesson here is; *100 percent code coverage does not have to be your goal*. Understanding your domain and the architecture of your application allows you to make much more reachable and realistic estimates for the amount of code coverage that:

- Gives you the confidence to change code without repercussions
- Gives you belief that the product you were asked to deliver, is the product you have created

Covering the exceptions

Continuing with our examination of the coverage report will lead us to discover another block that is not exercised by our current tests. The block in question is the last catch in the following try-catch block in app/TemperatureConverterActivity:

```
try {
    double temp = Double.parseDouble(str);
    double result = (option == Option.C2F)
? TemperatureConverter.celsiusToFahrenheit(temp)
: TemperatureConverter.fahrenheitToCelsius(temp);
    String resultString = String.format("%.2f",", ("%.("%.""," "
        result);
    destinationEditNumber.setNumber(result);
    destinationEditNumber.setSelection(resultString.length());
} catch (NumberFormatException ignore) {
// WARNING this is generated whilst numbers are being entered,
    // for example just a -''''''
    // so we don'tdon'tdon'tdon't' want to show the error just yet
} catch (Exception e) {
sourceEditNumber.setError("ERROR: " + e.getLocalizedMessage());
}
```

First things first, why are we catching generic Exception? Let's make this more specific to the error we are expecting to handle. That way we don't handle exceptions we aren't expecting, and also if someone reads the code they will know explicitly what we are trying to do here.

Now we know what code is causing us not to have full test coverage, we know what tests to write to throw this exception and update our test suite and our Jacoco report:

```
} catch (InvalidTemperatureException e) {
sourceEditNumber.setError("ERROR: " + e.getLocalizedMessage());
}
```

We should provide a test, or better a pair of tests, one for each temperature unit that given an invalid temperature verifies that the error is displayed. The following is the test in `TemperatureConverterActivityTests` for the Celsius case, and you can easily convert it to provide the Fahrenheit case:

```
public void testInvalidTemperatureInCelsius() throws Throwable {
        runTestOnUiThread(new Runnable() {
            @Override
            public void run() {
                celsiusInput.requestFocus();
            }
        });
        getInstrumentation().waitForIdleSync();

        // invalid temp less than ABSOLUTE_ZERO_C
        sendKeys("MINUS 3 8 0");");");");"

        String msg = "Expected celsius input to contain an
error.";.";.";.";"
        assertNotNull(msg, celsiusInput.getError());
}
```

We request the focus for the field under test. As we did before, we should achieve this by using a Runnable on the UI thread otherwise we will receive an exception.

Then set the invalid temperature and retrieve the error message to verify that it is not null. Running the end-to-end process again, we can attest that the path is now covered, giving us total coverage as intended.

This is the iterative process you should follow to change as much as possible of the code to green. As was said before, when the line of code is not green, as long as you have considered the options and are still confident in changing other code while this path is untested, then that is ok.

Introducing Robotium

One component of the vast emerging robotic fauna is Robotium (`http://robotium.org`), a test framework created to simplify the writing of tests, requiring minimal knowledge of the application under test. Robotium is mainly oriented to writing powerful and robust automatic black-box test cases for Android applications. It can cover function, system, and acceptance test scenarios, even spanning multiple Android activities of the same application automatically. Robotium can also be used to test applications that we don't have the source code for, or even pre-installed applications.

Let's put Robotium to work creating some new tests for `TemperatureConverter`. To keep our tests organized, we create a new package named `com.blundell.tut.robotium` in our `TemperatureConverter` project, under the `androidTest` directory. We will initially be testing `TemperatureConverterActivity`, it is reasonable to call it `TemperatureConverterActivityTests`, even though we already have a class with the same name in another package also extending `ActivityInstrumentationTestCase2`. After all, this class will contain tests for this same Activity too.

Adding Robotium

Let's add Robotium to our project, we'll only be using it in test cases and so it should go on the `testcase` classpath. As of this writing, the latest version of Robotium is 5.2.1. In `app/build.gradle`, we add the following:

```
dependencies {

    . . .

    androidTestCompile('com.jayway.android.robotium:robotium-
solo:5.2.1')
}
```

Creating the test cases

From the previous chapters, we know that if we are creating test cases for an Activity that should run connected to the system infrastructure, we should base it on `ActivityInstrumentationTestCase2`, and that is what we are going to do.

The testFahrenheitToCelsiusConversion() test

More or less the test cases have the same structure as other Instrumentation-based tests. The main difference is that we need to instantiate Robotium's Solo in the test `setUp()`, and clean up Robotium in the `tearDown()`:

```
public class TemperatureConverterActivityTests extends
ActivityInstrumentationTestCase2<TemperatureConverterActivity> {

    private TemperatureConverterActivity activity;
    private Solo solo;

    public TemperatureConverterActivityTests() {
        super(TemperatureConverterActivity.class);
    }

    @Override
    protected void setUp() throws Exception {
        super.setUp();
        activity = getActivity();
        solo = new Solo(getInstrumentation(), activity);
    }

    @Override
    protected void tearDown() throws Exception {
        solo.finishOpenedActivities();
        super.tearDown();
    }
}
```

To instantiate Solo, we have to pass a reference to the `Instrumentation` class and to the Activity under test.

On the other hand, to clean up Solo we should call the `finishOpenedActivities()` method. This will finalize Solo and then finish our Activity, and we then invoke `super.tearDown()`.

Solo provides a variety of methods to drive UI tests and some assertions. Let's start by re-implementing the `testFahrenheitToCelsiusConversion()` that we previously implemented using the conventional approach, but in this case using Solo facilities:

```
public void testFahrenheitToCelsiusConversion() {
solo.clearEditText(CELSIUS_INPUT);
    solo.clearEditText(FAHRENHEIT_INPUT);
```

```
    solo.clickOnEditText(FAHRENHEIT_INPUT);
    solo.enterText(FAHRENHEIT_INPUT, "32.5");
    solo.clickOnEditText(CELSIUS_INPUT);
    double f = 32.5;
    double expectedC = TemperatureConverter.fahrenheitToCelsius(f);
    double actualC =
((EditNumber) solo.getEditText(CELSIUS_INPUT)).getNumber();
    double delta = Math.abs(expectedC - actualC);

    String msg = f + "F -> " + expectedC + "C "
      + """""but was " + actualC + "C (delta " + delta + ")";
    assertTrue(msg, delta < 0.005);
}
```

This is pretty similar, however, the first difference you may have noticed is that in this case we are not getting references to the UI elements as we previously did in the `setUp()` method, using `findViewById()` to locate the view. However, we are using one of the biggest advantages of Solo, which is locating the views for us using some criteria. In this case, the criterion is the order in which the EditText appears. The `solo.clearEditText(int index)` method expects an integer index of the position on the screen starting from 0. Consequently, we should add these constants to the test case, just like in our user interface the Celsius field is on top, and Fahrenheit beneath:

```
    private static final int CELSIUS = 0;
    private static final int FAHRENHEIT = 1;
```

The other Robotium methods follow the same convention, and we are supplying these constants when necessary. This test is very similar to the one in `com.blundell.tut.TemperatureConverterActivityTest`, but you may have noticed that there is a subtle difference. Robotium is located at a much higher level and we don't have to worry about as many internals or implementation details; for example, when in our previous test we invoked `celciusInput.requestFocus()` to trigger the conversion mechanism, here we just simulate what the user does and issue a `solo.clickOnEditText(CELSIUS)`.

We simplified the test sensibly, but the biggest advantage of using Solo is yet to come.

Testing between Activities

As Robotium is situated at a much higher level, and we don't deal with implementation details, it is not our problem if a new Activity is launched when we click on an Android widget; we only treat this case from the UI perspective.

Here, I am going to discuss some functionality theoretically. This has not yet been created and is left up to the user as a further step, if you so wish.

Now that we have a working temperature converter, it would be nice if we could let the user decide up to how many decimal places they want to see a conversion. Allowing the user to change this option, via an Android Dialog, sounds like a sensible option.

Our purpose is to change the value of decimal places preference to five, and verify that the change actually took place. Because of the high level of Robotium, this test is readable and understandable without actually having the functionality implemented. This is an example of a BDD approach to implement this feature.

The following code snippet illustrates the details of the test:

```
public final void testClickOptionMenuSavesDecimalPreference() {
int decimalPlaces = 5;
    String numberRegEx = "^[0-9]+$";

    solo.sendKey(Solo.MENU);
    solo.clickOnText("Preferences");
    solo.clickOnText("Decimal places");
    assertTrue(solo.searchText(numberRegEx));

    solo.clearEditText(DECIMAL_PLACES);
    assertFalse(solo.searchText(numberRegEx));

    solo.enterText(DECIMAL_PLACES, Integer.toString(decimalPlaces));
solo.clickOnButton("OK");
    solo.goBack();

    solo.sendKey(Solo.MENU);
    solo.clickOnText("Preferences");
    solo.clickOnText("Decimal places");
    assertTrue(solo.searchText(numberRegEx));

    int editTextDecimalPlaces =
Integer.parseInt(solo.getEditText(DECIMAL_PLACES)
.getText().toString());
    assertEquals(decimalPlaces, editTextDecimalPlaces);
    }
```

There are no gory details about how shared preferences and options menus are implemented. We only test its functionality. We start by pressing the **MENU** key and clicking on **Preferences**.

Wow, we just specified the menu item title and that's it!

The new Activity has started, but we don't have to worry about that implementation detail. We continue and click on **Decimal places**.

We verify that some field containing a number, the prior value of this preference, appeared. Do you remember what I said about regular expressions? They always come in handy in one way or another, to match any decimal integer number (any digit followed by zero or more digits). Then, we clear the field and verify that it was in fact cleared.

We enter the string, representing the number we want to use as a preference, 5 in this case. Click on the **OK** button and the preference is saved.

Finally, we need to verify that it actually happened. The same procedure is used to get the menu and the field. Finally, we verify that the actual number is already there.

You may wonder where DECIMAL_PLACES come from. We previously defined CELSIUS and FAHRENHEIT index constants for the fields on the screen, and this is the same case, because this will be the third EditText we should define in our class:

```
private static final int DECIMAL_PLACES = 2;
```

Tests can be run from your IDE or the command line, according to your preferences.

Testing on the host's JVM

We left this subject for the end of this chapter, as it seems this is the *Holy Grail* of the Android platform.

Android is based on a virtual machine named **Dalvik**, after a village in Iceland, optimized for mobile resources with limited capabilities such as constrained amount of memory and processor speed. Thus representative of a mobile device but certainly a very different environment than our memory rich and speedy host computers, typically having plenty of memory and processor speed to enjoy.

Ordinarily, we run our applications and tests on an emulator or device. These targets have a much slower real or emulated CPU. Thus, running our tests is a time-consuming activity, mainly when our project starts to grow. Applying Test-driven Development techniques compels us to run hundreds of tests to verify every change we introduced.

It's worth noticing that this technique can be used only as a workaround during the development process to speed things up, and it should never replace final testing on the real platform, as incompatibilities between the Dalvik and JavaSE runtime may affect the accuracy of the tests.

We are half way there already with the creation of our core module. Now we are in the Java world and free to run our tests on the JVM (and use JUnit4, coming to an Android near you soon). There is one-way dependency from the app Android module to the core Java module. Allowing us to free ourselves from the shackles of Android testing, encumbrance when running tests in the core module.

Later, we should find out a method that allows us to intercept the standard compilation-dexing-running on an emulator or a device sequence, and be able to run Android on our host computer directly.

Comparing the performance gain

A quick reminder about the speed gain when running these Java-only tests compared to Android instrumentation tests.

The distinction is evident. There is no emulator start up, or any device communication, and therefore the speed gain is important. Analyzing the evidence, we can find out these differences.

Running all tests in my development computer takes 0.005 seconds; with some tests taking so little time that they are not even accounted for, and are displayed as 0.000 seconds.

If I move these tests to our app module, and run the same tests on the emulator, this makes the huge difference evident. These same tests took 0.443 seconds to run, almost 100 times more, and that's a huge difference if you consider hundreds of tests running, tens of times a day.

It is also good to notice that other advantages exist, besides the speed gain, and they are the availability of years of Java, tooling, library, and plugin creation, including several mock frameworks and code analysis tools.

Adding Android to the picture

We intentionally left Android outside our picture. Let's analyze what happens if we include a simple Android test inside `core`. Remember that for an Android test to compile `android.jar` from the SDK, it should also be added to the modules' libraries.

And here is what we obtain:

```
java.lang.RuntimeException: Stub!
    at android.content.Context.<init>(Context.java:4)
    at android.content.ContextWrapper.<init>(ContextWrapper.java:5)
    at android.app.Application.<init>(Application.java:6)
```

 Adding the `android.jar` to the class path for core is slightly awkward and longwinded. It is not something that is done by default. This is a good thing as it stops us accidentally using Android-specific classes when writing code inside core.

The reason is that `android.jar` provides only the API, not the implementation. All methods have the same implementation:

```
throw new RuntimeException("Stub!");
```

If we want to circumvent this limitation to test some classes outside of the Android operating system, we should create an `android.jar` that mocks every class. However, we would also find problems for subclasses of Android classes, like `TemperatureConverterApplication`. This would be a daunting task and a significant amount of work, so we should look for another solution.

Introducing Robolectric

Robolectric (`http://robolectric.org`) is a unit test framework that intercepts the loading of Android classes and rewrites the method bodies. Robolectric re-defines Android methods so they return default values, such as `null`, `0`, or `false`. If available, it forwards method calls to shadow objects, mimicking Android behavior.

A large number of shadow objects are provided, but this is far from complete coverage, however, it is improving constantly. This should also lead you to treat it as an evolving open source project, for which you should be ready to contribute to make it better, but also to depend on it with caution because you may discover that what you need for your tests has not been implemented yet. This is not in any way to diminish its existing prospects.

Installing Robolectric

Robolectric can be installed by using the latest Robolectric JAR from the Maven central repository. At the time of this writing, the latest available is version 2.4:

```
testCompile 'org.robolectric:robolectric:2.4'
```

Usually, adding a dependency is as simple as this one line, however, with Robolectric a bit of jiggery pokery is needed for it to work with the Gradle build types.

First, Robolectric tests require their own module to run in. This is nothing new. Create a new Java module, we'll call it `robolectric-tests`. Keep the package the same as always `com.blundell.tut`. Now, we have to modify the `robolectric-tests/build.gradle`, so we can hook Robolectric in place of the `android.jar`:

```
def androidModuleName = ":app";
def flavor = "debug"

evaluationDependsOn(androidModuleName)

apply plugin: 'java'

dependencies {
    def androidModule = project(androidModuleName)
    testCompile project(path: androidModuleName,
configuration: "${flavor}Compile")

    def debugVariant = androidModule.android.applicationVariants
.find({ it.name == flavor })
    testCompile debugVariant.javaCompile.classpath
    testCompile debugVariant.javaCompile.outputs.files
    testCompile files(
androidModule.plugins.findPlugin("com.android.application")
.getBootClasspath())

    testCompile 'junit:junit:4.12'
    testCompile 'org.robolectric:robolectric:2.4'
}
```

This is a big chunk of configuration to take in, let's break it down into steps.

Firstly, we define the module name for our Android application, and then we name the flavor that we will want to test against.

The `EvaluationDependsOn` class tells Gradle to ensure that our application module is evaluated before our tests, this stops any strange errors from order of execution quirks.

Next, we apply the java plugin as per normal convention for a Java project.

The dependencies closure is where we add all of the Android dependencies to our classpath. First, we add the selected build variant of our module, `debug`, then the classpath and its dependencies, also ensuring we have system dependencies from our Android plugin.

Lastly, we apply JUnit4 and Robolectric as test dependencies.

 Remember, if you have multiple product flavors and build types, then this configuration needs the full build variant adding to the script. It would be pretty straightforward to amend this build script.

Adding resources

When you run your tests, Robolectric attempts to look up your `AndroidManifest.xml` so it can find resources for your application, and know about your target SDK version, among other properties. With the current Robolectric version and our choice of using a separate module, Robolectric cannot find your resources or your Android manifest. You can still write tests and get feedback without this optional step, but you may find some strangeness when accessing classes that use resources; for example, `R.string.hello_world`, and will get messages like this in your console:

```
WARNING: No manifest file found at ./AndroidManifest.xml.Falling back to
the Android OS resources only. To remove this warning, annotate your test
class with @Config(manifest=Config.NONE).
```

This can be fixed by doing as it says with an `@Config` annotation, or creating a custom test runner that specifies the manifest location or as we choose to do here, creating a configuration file and adding it to your classpath. Inside the `robolectric-tests` module, create the folder `/src/test/resources`, and create a file `org.robolectric.Config.properties`. This will contain our Android manifest location; it will also contain our minimum SDK version, as we don't state this in our manifest. It will have these contents:

```
manifest=../app/src/main/AndroidManifest.xml
emulateSdk = 16
```

Robolectric attempts to look up your minimum SDK inside the `AndroidManifest.xml`. However, with the Gradle build system you do not declare it here, but declare it in the `app/build.gradle`.

We are now set up and ready to create some Robolectric tests!

Writing some tests

We will get acquainted with Robolectric by reproducing some of the tests we wrote before. One good example can be re-writing the `EditNumber` tests. Let's create a new `EditNumberTests` class, this time in the newly created project, and copy the tests from the `EditNumberTests` class in the `TemperatureConverterTest` project:

```
@RunWith(RobolectricTestRunner.class)
public class EditNumberTests {

    private static final double DELTA = 0.00001d;

    private EditNumber editNumber;
```

In the previous snippet, we declare the test runner with the `@RunWith` annotation. Then we defined the `editNumber` field, to hold the reference to the `EditNumber` class:

```
@Before
public void setUp() throws Exception {
    editNumber = new EditNumber(Robolectric.application);
    editNumber.setFocusable(true);
}
```

This snippet comprises the usual `setup()` method. In the `setUp()` method, we created an `EditNumber` with an application context, and then we set it as focusable. The context is used to create the view, and Robolectric handles this for us:

```
@Test
public final void testClear() {
    String value = "123.45";";";";"
    editNumber.setText(value);

    editNumber.clear();

    assertEquals("", editNumber.getText().toString());
}
```

```
@Test
public final void testSetNumber() {
    editNumber.setNumber(123.45);

    assertEquals("123.45", editNumber.getText().toString());
}

@Test
public final void testGetNumber() {
    editNumber.setNumber(123.45);

    assertEquals(123.45, editNumber.getNumber(), DELTA);
}
```

In this last snippet, we have the basic tests that are the same as the `EditNumber` tests of our previous examples.

We are highlighting the most important changes. The first one is to specify the test runner JUnit that will delegate the processing of the tests to, by using the annotation `@RunWith`. In this case, we need to use `RobolectricTestRunner.class` as the runner. Then we create an `EditText` class, using a Robolectric Context, as this is a class that couldn't be instantiated without some help. Finally, a `DELTA` value is specified in `testGetNumber` as `assertEquals` since, the floating point number requires it in JUnit 4. Additionally, we added the `@Test` annotation to mark the method as tests.

The other test methods that existed in the original `EditNumberTests` cannot be implemented, or simply fail for a variety of reasons. For example, as we mentioned before, Robolectric classes return default values, such as `null`, `0`, `false`, and so on, and this is the case for `Editable.Factory.getInstance()`, which returns null and causes the test to fail; because there is no other way of creating an `Editable` object, we are at a dead end.

Similarly, the `InputFilter` that `EditNumber` sets is non functional. It is futile to create a test that expects some behavior.

The alternative to these shortcomings would be to create `Shadow` classes, but this requires alteration of the Robolectric source and the creation of `Robolectric.shadowOf()` methods. This procedure is described in the documentation that you may follow, if you are interested in applying this approach to your tests.

Having identified these issues, we can proceed to run the tests, and they will run in the host's JVM with no need to start or communicate with an emulator or device.

Google's march on shadows

For some reason, Google does not *like* Robolectric, they've never acknowledged that it works, or never said that it's a solution to a problem. If they ignore the solution, then that means the problem of slow running tests doesn't exist, right. They seem to feel that Robolectric detracts from Android, and so have kind of publicly given it the cold shoulder. Surreptitiously pushing it away by ignoring its existence, that is up until now.

Google has created exactly what we said before, an `android.jar` file with default method implementations. This means no more `stub!` errors when accessing a method. Further, they have removed all of the `final` modifiers from classes, allowing mocking Frameworks to have a field day. Unfortunately, at the time of this writing it is undocumented. No surprise! I don't want to give usage steps, as while undocumented these will be changing rapidly. However, what I will say is, if Google got this right, then it means for the testing scenario described previously, Robolectric is out of the window, and we can use the standard Android testing SDKs. The same principles will apply, and so I think it's still valuable if you understand how Robolectric works. You can apply this understanding to the future that I cannot.

Introducing Fest

Another weapon for our testing arsenal is better testing assertions. Have you noticed how sometimes stacktraces for failed tests are really unfriendly and/or mystically wrong? They give you little information about the real failure and you end up confused, having to read the entire source to fathom out how to fix the problem.

As an example, look at this assertion:

```
org.junit.Assert.assertEquals(3, myList.size());
```

We are asserting that a collection of objects after some task has a size of three, look at our error message when the test fails:

```
java.lang.AssertionError:
Expected :3
Actual   :2
```

Ok, that kind of makes sense, but it's a bit abstract. What item is missing from our list? I am going to have to run the tests again to find out, or I could add a custom error message:

```
assertEquals("List not the correct size " + myList,
3, myList.size());
```

Giving me the error message:

```
java.lang.AssertionError: List not the correct size [A, B]
Expected :3
Actual   :2
```

That error message is much better. It shows I'm missing C from my list. However, looking back at the assertion, it's getting kind of unreadable. Sometimes, at a glance, it might even appear like I am trying to assert whether that initial string is equal to the other vars, the parameter ordering does not help at all. What if I had another object that doesn't so easily implement toString? I would need to create more custom code to print a nice error message, probably repeating myself quite a lot with boiler plate error messages.

Stop all that worrying right now! Take a look at how we can do the same assertion with Fest:

```
org.fest.assertions.api.assertThat(myList).hasSize(3);
```

Now, our error message looks like:

```
java.lang.AssertionError: expected size:<3> but was:<2> in:<['A',
'B'']>
```

Nice, with no extra effort by us, we get an error message showing us what is in the list and how the sizes differentiate. Also looking back at the assertion, it's much more readable and even coding it was easier with the fluid interface. This improves the readability of our test code, and speeds up debugging and test fixing.

After doing this change, I came to realize we actually might have wanted to test the contents of the List, but due to the encumbrance of the JUnit assertions, we were not bothering. Fest to the rescue once more:

```
assertThat(myList).contains("A", ""B", ""C");
output:
  java.lang.AssertionError: expecting:
<['A',]>
 to contain:
<['A', 'B', 'C']>
 but could not find:
<['C']>
```

Think how we would have had to do that with JUnit assertions, and I think you'll appreciate the power of Fest.

Fest comes in multiple flavors for assertions on different libraries; these include the java flavor, as shown previously, and an Android flavor, which allows you to do fluid-style interface assertions on Android components, like Views and Fragments. Here is an example of JUnit asserting visibility, and then Fest:

```
assertEquals(View.VISIBLE, layout.getVisibility());
```

```
assertThat(layout).isVisible();
```

Adding either library to your project is just another Gradle dependency, the latest versions can be found on Maven central. Here is the example for Java fest, the latest at the time of writing:

```
testCompile 'org'.easytesting:fest-assert-core:2.0M10'
```

Note, that Android Fest has been rebranded into Assert-J and is split into many dependencies depending on what you want to test. The assertions will work exactly the same way. More information and instructions to add as a dependency can be found at https://github.com/square/assertj-android.

Introducing Spoon

Device fragmentation is always talked about around Android and it is something you should be considerate of. The number of different devices and form factors means you really need to be confident that your application runs well, on all the aforementioned. Spoon is right here to help; Spoon (http://square.github.io/spoon) is an open-source project that gives you a test runner that allows instrumentation tests to be run on all connected devices in parallel. It also allows you to take screenshots as the tests are running. Not only does this speed up your testing and feedback cycle, it also allows you to potentially visually see where tests went wrong.

Spoon can be added to your project with this dependency:

```
testCompile com.squareup.spoon:spoon-client:1.1.2
```

You can then take screenshots inside your tests, allowing you to see the state of your application when you are also asserting behavior:

```
Spoon.screenshot(activity, "max_celcius_to_fahrenheit");
```

If you take the screenshot right before your assertion, you can use the screenshots to help you determine failures. Another cool feature is Spoon will collate your screenshots from one test into an animated GIF. so you can watch the sequence of events.

Spoon is then run from the command line, using this command:

```
$java -jar spoon-runner-1.1.2-jar-with-dependencies.jar \
    --apk androidApplicationTestGuide.apk \
--test-apk androidApplicationTestGuideTests.apk
```

 You can find your APK files inside the /build/ folder. If you need more information of using the APK files in this way, and testing from the command line, take a look back at *Chapter 7, Behavior-driven Development*.

Introducing Fork

Another humorous name for a library, but stick with it reader, this similarity is not just a co-incidence. After telling you how amazing Spoon is at speeding up your tests by running all your instrumentation tests in parallel on all connected devices, well here comes Fork, to tell you that this naïve scheduling (their words not mine), is a burden on yourself and your CI. Fork can run your tests even faster!

Fork increases your tests' speed by introducing a concept called **Device Pools**. In simple terms, imagine you had two identical devices, which are two Sony Xperia Z1s running Android 5.0. Fork will take your test suite and split it in half, running half the tests on each device. Thus, it saves you 50 percent of the test run speed (roughly excluding warm up/setup time).

These device pools come in different flavors for things such as, api level, smallest width, tablet devices, or manual pools, where you declare the device serial id you want to use. More information about device pools and custom parameters for the fork task can be found at http://goo.gl/cIm6GQ.

Fork can be used with Gradle, by adding the plugin to your build script and applying it:

```
buildscript {
    dependencies {
        classpath 'com'.shazam.fork:fork-gradle-plugin:0.10.0'
    }
}

apply plugin: 'fork'
```

Now, you can run fork tests instead of your normal instrumentation tests with this command:

```
./gradlew fork
```

 If you have multiple flavors in your project, you can see what fork tasks are available with the command: `./gradlew tasks | grep fork`.

Spoon and Fork are powerful tools, and combined now with your knowledge of instrumentation tests, unit testing, benchmarking, and code analysis, you can put together a robust, informational, and well-rounded test suite, which gives you confidence and agility when it comes to writing your Android applications.

Summary

This chapter has been a little more involved than previous ones, with the sole intention of facing realistic situations and state-of-the-art Android testing.

We started by enabling code coverage through Jacoco, running our tests, and obtaining a detailed code coverage analysis report.

We then used this report to improve our test suite. Writing tests to cover code we were not aware had not been tested. This led us to better tests, and in some cases improved the design of the project under test.

We introduced Robotium, a very useful tool to ease the creation of test cases for our Android applications, and we improved some tests with it.

Then we analyzed one of the hottest topics in Android testing; testing on the development host JVM, optimizing, and reducing considerably the time needed to run the tests. Something that is highly desirable when we are applying Test-driven Development to our process. Within this scope, we analyzed Robolectric and created some tests as demonstrations to get you started on these techniques.

To round off our knowledge, we looked at Fest and some cutlery these can help us have more expressive tests, improved feedback, and a more powerful overall test suite.

We have reached the end of this journey through the available methods and tools for Android testing. You should now be much better prepared to start applying this to your own projects. The results will be visible as soon as you begin to use them.

Finally, I hope that you have enjoyed reading this book as much as I did writing it.

Happy testing!

Index

A

AccessPrivateDataTest class 64
activities
  testing 64-71
ActivityInstrumentationTestCase2 class
  about 56
  constructor 56
  setUp method 56, 57
  tearDown method 57
ActivityInstrumentationTestCase2.get
      Activity() method 141
Activity Manager
  URL 16
ActivityMonitor inner class
  about 50
  example 50, 51
ActivityTestCase class
  about 54, 55
  scrubClass method 55
Android
  unit tests 63, 64
Android applications
  building manually, Gradle used 116-119
Android developer guide
  URL 193
Android Emulator plugin 121
Android project
  creating 17, 18
  package, exploring 19
  test annotations 22, 23
  test case, creating 20-22
  tests, debugging 31
  tests, running 23
Android SDK
  performance tests 198

Android Studio
  support, for system tests 13
  tests, running 23, 24
AndroidTestCase base class
  about 46
  assertActivityRequiresPermission()
      method 46
  assertWritingContentUriRequires
      Permission() method 48
Android testing framework
  about 14
  features 14
  Gradle 16
  instrumentation framework 15, 16
  test targets 17
android-test-kit
  URL 96
android.test.mock subpackage
  MockApplication class 42
  MockContentProvider class 42
  MockContentResolver class 42
  MockContext class 43
  MockCursor class 43
  MockDialogInterface class 43
  MockPackageManager class 43
  MockResources class 43
Android Virtual Devices. See **AVD**
annotations, tests
  @FlakyTest 22
  @LargeTest 22
  @MediumTest 22
  @SmallTest 22
  @Smoke 22
  @Suppress 23
  @UIThreadTest 23
  about 22

URL 14
used, for building Android applications
    manually 116-119
used, for running tests 29
Gradle Jacoco plugin
    URL 218
GraphViz
    URL 206

H

HAXM
    AVD, speeding up with 105, 106
headless emulator 99, 100

I

instrumentation
    about 15, 16, 49
    ActivityMonitor inner class 50
InstrumentationTestCase class
    about 51
    launchActivity method 52
    launchActivityWithIntent method 52
    runTestOnUiThread helper method 54
    sendKeys method 52, 53
    sendRepeatedKeys method 52, 53
integration tests
    about 9
    UI tests 10
IsolatedContext class 43

J

Jacoco
    about 216
    coverage report 220
    features 216, 217
    URL 2
Java testing framework 14
jbehave
    about 11
    URL 11
Jenkins
    about 121
    Android test results, obtaining 126-128

configuring 121, 122
installing 121, 122
jobs, creating 122-125
URL 121
JUnit plugin 121
Jython
    URL 109

K

keyguard
    disabling 101

L

LaunchPerformanceBase instrumentation
    creating 198, 199
libraries
    using 60, 61
local and remote services
    testing 80, 81

M

macrobenchmarks 209
memory usage
    testing for 91-93
microbenchmarks
    about 209
    Caliper 209
micro-optimizations 194
MockContentResolver class 44
MockContext class 43
Mockito
    about 82
    benefits 82
    URL 81
    usage example 83
mock objects
    about 8, 9, 42
    alternate route, providing to database
        operations 44
    alternate route, providing to file 44
    EditNumber filter tests 83-87
    IsolatedContext class 43
    libraries, importing 83
    MockContentResolver class 44

Thank you for buying
Learning Android Application Testing

About Packt Publishing

Packt, pronounced 'packed', published its first book, *Mastering phpMyAdmin for Effective MySQL Management*, in April 2004, and subsequently continued to specialize in publishing highly focused books on specific technologies and solutions.

Our books and publications share the experiences of your fellow IT professionals in adapting and customizing today's systems, applications, and frameworks. Our solution-based books give you the knowledge and power to customize the software and technologies you're using to get the job done. Packt books are more specific and less general than the IT books you have seen in the past. Our unique business model allows us to bring you more focused information, giving you more of what you need to know, and less of what you don't.

Packt is a modern yet unique publishing company that focuses on producing quality, cutting-edge books for communities of developers, administrators, and newbies alike. For more information, please visit our website at www.packtpub.com.

About Packt Open Source

In 2010, Packt launched two new brands, Packt Open Source and Packt Enterprise, in order to continue its focus on specialization. This book is part of the Packt Open Source brand, home to books published on software built around open source licenses, and offering information to anybody from advanced developers to budding web designers. The Open Source brand also runs Packt's Open Source Royalty Scheme, by which Packt gives a royalty to each open source project about whose software a book is sold.

Writing for Packt

We welcome all inquiries from people who are interested in authoring. Book proposals should be sent to author@packtpub.com. If your book idea is still at an early stage and you would like to discuss it first before writing a formal book proposal, then please contact us; one of our commissioning editors will get in touch with you.

We're not just looking for published authors; if you have strong technical skills but no writing experience, our experienced editors can help you develop a writing career, or simply get some additional reward for your expertise.

Android Application Testing Guide

ISBN: 978-1-84951-350-0   Paperback: 332 pages

Build intensively tested and bug free Android applications

1. The first and only book that focuses on testing Android applications.

2. Step-by-step approach clearly explaining the most efficient testing methodologies.

3. Real world examples with practical test cases that you can reuse.

Robotium Automated Testing for Android

ISBN: 978-1-78216-801-0   Paperback: 94 pages

Efficiently automate test cases for Android applications using Robotium

1. Integrate Robotium with Maven to perform test case execution during build.

2. Learn different steps to connect to a remote client from an android using Robotium.

3. Understand the benefits of Robotium over other test frameworks.

Please check **www.PacktPub.com** for information on our titles

[PACKT] PUBLISHING   open source✿
community experience distilled

Testing and Securing Android
Studio Applications

Debug and secure your Android applications with Android Studio

Belén Cruz Zapata
Antonio Hernández Niñirola   [PACKT] open source✿

Testing and Securing Android Studio Applications

ISBN: 978-1-78398-880-8   Paperback: 162 pages

Debug and secure your Android applications with Android Studio

1. Explore the foundations of security and learn how to apply these measures to create secure applications using Android Studio.

2. Create effective test cases, unit tests, and functional tests to ensure your Android applications function correctly.

3. Optimize the performance of your app by debugging and using high-quality code.

Android Development
Tools for Eclipse

Set up, build, and publish Android projects quickly using Android Development Tools for Eclipse

Sanjay Shah
Khirulnizam Abd Rahman   [PACKT] open source✿

Android Development Tools for Eclipse

ISBN: 978-1-78216-110-3   Paperback: 144 pages

Set up, build, and publish Android projects quickly using Android Development Tools for Eclipse

1. Build Android applications using ADT for Eclipse.

2. Generate Android application skeleton code using wizards.

3. Advertise and monetize your applications.

Please check **www.PacktPub.com** for information on our titles

Printed in Great Britain
by Amazon